D1566025

ELEANOR ROOSEVELT:

RELUCTANT FIRST LADY

Also by Lorena A. Hickok

THE TOUCH OF MAGIC:
The Story of Helen Keller's Great Teacher, Anne Sullivan Macy

ELEANOR ROOSEVELT: RELUCTANT FIRST LADY

By LORENA A. HICKOK

Introduction by Allen Klots

ILLUSTRATED WITH PHOTOGRAPHS

DODD, MEAD & COMPANY • NEW YORK

1   2   3   4   5   6   7   8   9   10

Library of Congress Cataloging in Publication Data

Hickok, Lorena A
    Eleanor Roosevelt, reluctant First Lady.

    Published in 1962 under title: Reluctant First Lady.
    1. Roosevelt, Eleanor Roosevelt, 1884-1962.
2. Presidents—United States—Wives—Biography.
3. Hickok, Lorena A.   I. Title.
E807.1.R48H52   1980   973.917′092′4 [B]   79-26769
ISBN 0-396-07836-2

One day quite a few years ago, one of Mrs. Roosevelt's grandsons, then aged five, asked the late Malvina Thompson, her secretary:

"Tommy, who is Grandmère?"

"Why, she's your grandmother, of course," Tommy replied.

"I know that," he said patiently, "but who is she? Daddy listens to what she says. You do what she tells you to do. Everybody stands up when she comes in. Who *is* Grandmère?"

To that little boy, now a young man, and to all her other grandchildren, this book is dedicated, with affection.

Acknowledgments

The story in this book is a very personal one. It had to be. For it was written largely out of the memories of two persons—Mrs. Roosevelt's and mine. This is especially true of our vacation motor trips, since on those trips we were alone or with strangers most of the time. Neither of us ever kept any notes or diaries.

Neither Mrs. Roosevelt's memory nor mine is infallible, of course. A great deal of checking had to be done. And for that I am deeply indebted to the staff of the Franklin D. Roosevelt Library. This book could not have been written without their help. I should like to express my gratitude to Miss Elizabeth B. Drewry, Director of the Roosevelt Library; Raymond H. Corry, Curator of the Museum; Joseph W. Marshall, Librarian; Miss Margaret L. Suckley, Archivist, who found most of the pictures; Jerome V. Deyo, Archivist; William F. Stickle, Staff Photographer, who copied the pictures;

and Mrs. Clarice D. Morris, Secretary to the Director. No matter what I asked for—and some of it required some hard searching, I'm sure—they always found it.

I want to give special thanks to Mrs. Anne S. Morris, Library Assistant. The most accurate source for material for this book was The New York *Times*. The Roosevelt Library has bound volumes of the *Times,* starting before President Roosevelt's first inauguration and ending sometime after his death. The volumes are big and heavy, and the print is fine. Because of some eye difficulty, I could not read them. The weather while this book was being written was hot and humid most of the time. The *Times* volumes are kept in the attic of the Roosevelt Library, and the heat up there must have been almost beyond endurance. Never a week went by when I did not call once or twice and ask for some date, a name, a quotation from one of my own stories, written while I was covering Mrs. Roosevelt. And it was nearly always Mrs. Morris who went up there, dragged out one of those heavy volumes and phoned back to me the information I needed. When I apologized for all the trouble I was giving her, her answer was always the same, a cheerful "That's what I'm here for." Thanking her this way isn't really adequate—but I mean it, from the bottom of my heart.

I also wish to thank a thirteen-year-old girl, my friend, Sandra de Vries, who spent one long summer day in a hot, stuffy dark room at the Adriance Memorial Library, in Poughkeepsie, reading aloud to me, from microfilm, stories I had written about Mrs. Roosevelt that had appeared in the *Poughkeepsie New Yorker*. She refused to take the pay I offered her. Many of the quotations in the early chapters are taken from those stories.

My agent, Miss Nannine Joseph, has, as always, been much more than an agent—a thoughtful, constructive critic. And any writer must find it a pleasure to work with my editor, Allen Klots, Jr. Also there is Jean Taylor Hartwig, who copied the manuscript for me, in very hot, disagreeable weather, with a husband, a baby and a house to look after, too. Again and again, after I had turned the manuscript over to her, I'd think of changes —substituting a word or a sentence here, inserting a paragraph there. I'd dictate them to her over the telephone. She never complained—and she never got them mixed up either!

Finally there is Mrs. Roosevelt herself. To her I can only say, after a friendship that has lasted nearly thirty years, "Thank you, my dear, for some of the happiest and most memorable days of my whole life!"

LORENA A. HICKOK
Hyde Park, N.Y.
1962

Grateful acknowledgment is made to the Franklin D. Roosevelt Library for their assistance in providing prints of all the illustrations in this 1980 edition of *Eleanor Roosevelt: Reluctant First Lady.*

ALLEN KLOTS

Introduction: Some Memories of Hick

I met Lorena Hickok, known to her friends as "Hick," when I edited the first book that she published with Dodd, Mead & Company, a biography of Anne Sullivan Macy entitled *The Touch of Magic*. She was then living at Hyde Park where one of her neighbors was Eleanor Roosevelt, a friend for almost thirty years, and this eventually led to discussion of a book that Hick proposed to write about Mrs. Roosevelt.

Hick was an impressive person in many ways. She was as large in spirit as she was physically. By the time I knew her in the early sixties, she was already much afflicted. Her eyesight was failing, and she wore glasses with heavy black rims surrounding thick, strong lenses. She had great pain in her legs, which made it agony to transport her considerable weight, even with the aid of canes. But she had enormous courage and rarely complained except to apologize for moving so slowly. She smoked incessantly, cigarettes and an occasional cigar, exuding clouds of smoke as though fueled by a highly inefficient coal furnace. As is often the case for smokers with poor vision, the ashes that dropped from her cigarettes formed a coat of dust on her clothes. She was externally untidy, but she had a well-organized, informed mind, and she said what she thought.

It was not hard to see in her the qualities of honesty, bravery, and wisdom that must have appealed to Mrs. Roosevelt, despite the difference in background between the patrician from New York and the rough-hewn journalist from East Troy, Wisconsin. Nothing was too much trouble for Mrs. Roosevelt to ease Hick's way. It was in Mrs. Roosevelt's car, driven by herself or alone with a chauffeur, for example, that Hick was brought to New York from Hyde Park. As the story of their friendship unfolded to me, I had the sense that the solicitude on Mrs. Roosevelt's part for Hick in those later days was unspoken gratitude for the comfort that Hick had given the First Lady during her loneliness at the time of their first meeting.

They had met when Hick was an active and imaginative reporter for the Associated Press. She had been assigned to cover the wife of New York's governor in October 1932, when it was becoming increasingly apparent that he would be the next President of the United States. Mrs. Roosevelt had been raised in an era when it was thought improper for a lady's name to appear in the press, unless in a society column, and her first encounter with a female reporter following her every move was an uneasy one. Hick's sympathy and native common sense, however, quickly made it evident that she would not abuse the privileges granted to her, and her intelligent awareness of the world around her made her a stimulating companion. Thus the basis was formed for the extraordinary friendship that was to enrich their lives for the rest of their days.

With the encouragement of Mrs. Roosevelt, Hick was inspired to tell the story of the first years of their friendship during Mrs. Roosevelt's adjustment from civilian to First Lady. I recall Hick telling me that one of the aspects of this project that Mrs. Roosevelt found attractive was the fact that the story could depend upon their own recollections and did not require exhaustive research that would tire Hick's eyes. Mrs. Roosevelt's unselfish willingness to share her reminiscences so freely with Hick was, of course, characteristic of the lengths to which she would go to help her friend. Neither of them had kept notes of their experiences and trips together, so that the narrative to be told had to come directly from the memories of each of them.

And what memories they were. At the outset, Mrs. Roosevelt had been overwhelmed by a sense of inadequacy in carrying out her new responsibilities as First Lady of the Land and mistress of the White House, particularly when she compared herself, as she could not help doing, with some of the more successful First Ladies, such as Edith, wife of her uncle Theodore. She was also desperate to preserve some of her independence which was so important to her. Consequently, during the momentous days of the campaign, election, and inauguration, she found herself increasingly alone. As she remarked to Hick, "I never wanted to be a President's wife, and I don't want it now. . . . Now I shall have to work out my own salvation. I'm afraid it may be a little difficult." In these moments of loneliness, she turned repeatedly to Hick, who was always nearby or at her side and whose responsiveness and discretion could be relied upon. Thus, they were together at such times as election day night, on inauguration eve when they read the various drafts of the President's speech, and for Hick's last interview as a reporter, exclusively given in the White House on Mrs. Roosevelt's return from the inauguration ceremony. It was the President's wife who arranged for Hick to become confidential investigator of poverty areas for Harry Hopkins, the Federal Relief Administrator, and she was a frequent guest at the White House, as part of what Mrs. Roosevelt called "the people in the house." And it was Hick whom the reluctant First Lady chose to accompany her alone during the first two summers on the trips in which she made a valiant but futile effort to prove that she could preserve her privacy as the wife of the President.

During the preparation of this book which tells that story, I had frequent meetings with Hick to which I always looked forward. Despite her difficulty in moving around, she insisted upon coming to the office at first. Eventually, I was able to persuade her to restrict our meetings to circumstances more convenient to her such as lunches in a hotel on Forty-second Street where she would stay, and their timing would depend upon when Mrs. Roosevelt's car was available to transport her. Hick

was a fascinating raconteur. After lunch, she would
sometimes replace the eternal cigarette with a cigar
while she reminisced. In her recollections it was apparent what a good newspaperwoman she had been and
what a useful reporter to Harry Hopkins, or indeed, to
the President. One could be sure that when she went
to the desolate communities of West Virginia in the
darkest days of the depression, for example, she had
spoken the language of the miners, and her stories of
those times never lost her dry wit.

In talking to Hick about Mrs. Roosevelt, we hit upon
an idea for a book that Hick agreed might appeal to
her and, with the support of their literary agent and
old friend Nannine Joseph, Hick undertook to present
it to her. The project was simply to collect Mrs. Roosevelt's favorite writings devoted to Christmas into a
volume that would be called *Eleanor Roosevelt's Christmas Book*. Mrs. Roosevelt liked the proposal and
promptly volunteered her own descriptions of Christmas at Hyde Park and in the White House, as well as
an original Christmas story.

A happy consequence of my involvement with Hick
on *Reluctant First Lady* and with Mrs. Roosevelt on her
Christmas book was, for me, a memorable lunch to
which Mrs. Roosevelt invited me with Hick and Nannine Joseph. Knowing my eagerness to meet Mrs. Roosevelt, Hick had urged her that she should extend this
invitation to me as the co-conspirator on the Christmas
book who had also been the editor closely associated
with *Reluctant First Lady*. At that time, Mrs. Roosevelt
had suddenly become preoccupied with the round-the-

clock meetings of the committee responsible for negotiating the exchange of farm tractors for American prisoners captured at the Bay of Pigs in Cuba, and I was alerted by Hick to expect the lunch to be canceled. But Mrs. Roosevelt was not to disappoint her friends even with such provocation.

I remember arriving at Mrs. Roosevelt's apartment promptly to find Hick and Nannine already there. Mrs. Roosevelt made me feel immediately at home so that I forgot instantly the world problems with which she was concerned and any embarrassment I might have had about frivolously distracting her from them. Our hostess declared that, in celebration of the gathering and the book, she would make an exception and have an aperitif with us before lunch. I recall that apartment as a modest one, all the more welcoming for being so, with the clutter of family memorabilia that one might expect. During a delicious lunch of lamb chops and raspberries fresh from the garden at Hyde Park, Mrs. Roosevelt apologetically turned at the table to proofs of captions for illustrations of her next book which had to be sent back that day. She discussed them with us, and somehow this interruption only served to enhance the informality and warmth of the occasion. Then, with the raspberries, there was unexpectedly brought in a simple homemade cake with a single lighted candle. With a rousing chorus of "Happy Birthday" from Mrs. Roosevelt, Hick, and belatedly me, it was placed before a beaming Nannine, revealing the well-kept secret that it was her birthday, which our hostess had not forgotten. I had the comfortable sense of being made a party to a gathering of three old friends together.

In her final years, Hick was endeavoring to complete a biography of Walter Reuther. It had been Mrs. Roosevelt who had introduced her to Reuther one weekend when he visited Hyde Park. My meetings with Hick continued in connection with this book, but they became fewer and fewer. She grew increasingly disabled and missed all the more the aid and comfort that had been given to her by Mrs. Roosevelt, who had died in 1962, shortly after *Reluctant First Lady* had been published. Hick never lost the discipline of a good journalist and was impatient and apologetic about the delays necessitated by her physical handicaps. In what turned out to be her last letter to me, she wrote that she was training "to work over an aching back as professional singers train themselves to sing over a heavy chest cold."

She could no longer travel to Detroit to interview the Reuther family, and, in what must have been a tribute to her courage, the busy Reuther brothers would arrange to see her on their hectic visits to New York. It was when she made the supreme effort to come down for one of these meetings with a Reuther, in a hired car from Hyde Park, that I saw her for the last time. She died shortly thereafter in 1968.

I shall never forget that last vision of Hick as she entered the dining room of the hotel where we met in New York. Now almost blind, she nevertheless insisted upon making her way independently. It seemed forever, as she moved at a snail's pace with the aid of two canes, each step an expression of the agony she must have felt.

And then when she finally came to rest and began to talk through the cigarette smoke, one was reminded of the extraordinary vigor that made her the first-rate journalist she was and endeared her to that great lady of the twentieth century, Eleanor Roosevelt.

ALLEN KLOTS
New York, N.Y.
1980

Contents

Illustrations

On the summer night in 1932 when Governor Franklin D. Roosevelt of New York won the Democratic nomination for President, reporters, photographers, newsreel men—along with his friends and well-wishers—swarmed all over the old Executive Mansion in Albany. Some of the reporters went looking for Mrs. Roosevelt.

They found her in the kitchen, cooking scrambled eggs for her husband, who had had no dinner. It was nearly midnight. She was wearing a pale green chiffon hostess gown, and she somehow managed not to get a single spot on it.

One of the more enthusiastic girl reporters gushed:

"Mrs. Roosevelt, aren't you thrilled at the idea of living in the White House?"

Mrs. Roosevelt did not answer. She merely looked at the girl. And the expression on her face, almost angry, stopped all questions along that line.

It puzzled me, but I finally concluded that she had merely thought it was a stupid question. Yet I wasn't quite sure.

1

Train Ride to Albany

"IF I WANTED to be selfish, I could wish Franklin had not been elected."

Mrs. Franklin D. Roosevelt, wife of the newly elected President of the United States, gazed out the train window at the Hudson River, gray and misty under slanting sheets of rain. Her expression was wistful—and a little guilty.

"Well, anyway, you'll be First Lady," her companion observed. And felt foolish after making the remark.

"I suppose they'll call me that," Mrs. Roosevelt replied with a sigh.

Then she added emphatically:

"But there isn't going to be any First Lady. There is just going to be plain, ordinary Mrs. Roosevelt. And that's all."

As a reporter for the Associated Press, I had been assigned to cover Mrs. Roosevelt in October, when the political experts decided that her husband would probably be elected. That November afternoon I was accompanying Mrs. Roosevelt to Albany to get an interview en route.

We were riding in a day coach. It would never have occurred to Mrs. Roosevelt to take a seat in the parlor car on a trip between New York and Albany or Hyde Park.

Mrs. Roosevelt continued to gaze out the window.

"I never wanted it," she said, "even though some people have said that my ambition for myself drove him on. They've even said that I had some such idea in the back of my mind when I married him. I never wanted to be a President's wife, and I don't want it now."

She glanced at me with a slight smile.

"You don't quite believe me, do you?" she asked. "Very likely no one would—except some woman who has had the job."

She was mistaken. I did believe her. For weeks we had been together almost constantly, the reporter dogging her footsteps day in and day out. It had been a little difficult at first, for Mrs. Roosevelt was extremely shy, especially with reporters. Not with the political writers, who covered her husband, but with the reporters who covered her—or tried to. The fact that this particular reporter had been a political writer covering her husband before she was assigned to take on Mrs. Roosevelt might help some, I had hoped. Thrown together as we were, we would have become mortal enemies or very good friends. We had become very good friends. I was now fairly well aware of how Mrs. Roosevelt felt about what

lay ahead of her, although she had never talked so
frankly about it before.

"For him, of course, I'm glad—sincerely," Mrs. Roosevelt added after a pause. "I couldn't have wanted it to
go the other way. After all, I'm a Democrat, too.

"Now I shall have to work out my own salvation. I'm
afraid it may be a little difficult. I know what Washington is like. I've lived there."

For eight years, during the administration of President
Wilson, her husband had been Assistant Secretary of
the Navy. They had not been very happy years for Mrs.
Roosevelt.

Almost defiantly, she continued:

"I shall very likely be criticized. But I can't help it."

Mrs. Roosevelt, when her husband was elected Presi-
dent, held two jobs. She taught at the Todhunter School
for Girls in New York, of which she was part owner.
And she was editor of a magazine called *Babies—Just
Babies,* a Bernarr McFadden publication. Most of the
McFadden publications were not the sort with which a
President's wife could be expected to be associated.

She said she would be giving up her teaching job on
March 1, three days before the inauguration, which that
year for the last time was held on March 4.

"I hate to do it," she said, shaking her head. "I wonder if you have any idea how I hate to do it."

I thought I knew. The celebration at the Democratic
National Headquarters at the Biltmore Hotel on election night had been crowded, jubilant and prolonged.
But at 8:30 the next morning we met at the Roosevelt
town house, on East 65th Street, and went to the school,

where at nine o'clock she held her first morning class. We were accompanied by her little blonde grandchild, Sistie, Anna's daughter, who had recently entered the first grade.

Mrs. Roosevelt's pupils were girls of high school age, studying American history. They sat around a table, as college students do in a seminar course. The atmosphere usually must have been friendly and informal.

That morning the girls all stood up as Mrs. Roosevelt entered, and one of them made a shy little speech about how pleased they were to have the First Lady of the Land for their teacher.

Mrs. Roosevelt looked embarrassed as she thanked the speaker and motioned for the class to be seated. Her expression was sad, as she said softly:

"But I haven't changed inside. I'm just the same as I was yesterday."

Now she turned away from the train window and said earnestly:

"I've liked teaching more than anything else I've ever done. But it's got to go. Perhaps sometimes some of the girls can come down to see me in Washington."

For years—until our entry into World War II made it too difficult—the graduating class of the Todhunter School was invited each year to spend a spring weekend at the White House as Mrs. Roosevelt's guests.

She did not tell her pupils that morning that after a few more weeks she could not be their teacher.

Mrs. Roosevelt's expression was determined as she continued:

"The job with the magazine I shall keep. That contract was signed months ago, with my husband's consent. I have the absolute say as to what goes into it—advertising as well as editorial material.

"I went into it because I wanted money. I have a small income of my own, but I need more money to do a lot of things I like to do. They're not important things at all—just things that give me fun."

Louis McHenry Howe, Franklin Roosevelt's long-time intimate friend, had told me that the thing that gave Mrs. Roosevelt the most fun was giving money away. Not in large sums to organized charities—although in later years in the White House, when her earnings were very large, she gave huge sums to the American Friends Service Committee and, during World War II, to the American Red Cross. But in the days before she went to the White House she liked to give money directly to people who needed it. Sometimes, Louis said, the gift would run into hundreds of dollars. Sometimes it would be a five-dollar bill. On herself she spent little. On a recent trip to Boston she had worn a dress that cost ten dollars.

Mrs. Roosevelt smiled as an amusing thought occurred to her.

"Sometimes," she said, "I daresay I shall feel a little as one of my boys felt, after I had lectured him on the responsibilities incumbent on the son of a man in public life. He said: 'Wouldn't it be fun to do things just because you wanted to do them?' "

She opened her bulging brief case and took out a folder filled with papers—the homework of some of her pupils.

"A teacher also has homework to do," she explained, as she drew out a pencil and started to read, at times frowning a little as she made a marginal correction, at times smiling at some mistake that amused her.

It was twilight when we arrived in Albany. We walked through the station together. The rain had stopped.

"I'm going to walk," Mrs. Roosevelt announced, waving away a cab driver who reached for her brief case.

It is probably two miles from the railroad station to the Executive Mansion, starting with a climb up a steep hill toward the Capitol.

"Isn't that brief case heavy?" I asked.

"No," Mrs. Roosevelt replied, "and I need the exercise."

From the entrance to the station I watched her set out with her long, swinging stride across the plaza toward the hill. Then I went back into the station, had a sandwich and a cup of coffee and took the next train back to New York.

I had a story to write—a good story. But it worried me. I knew she meant what she said. She was not going to be First Lady in the generally accepted sense of the term. In effect, she was serving notice on the American public not to expect her to be the sheltered, conventional White House mistress to which it was accustomed and of which it approved. And she had given me permission to quote her.

"She's letting herself in for trouble," I thought.

2

First Impressions

THE FIRST TIME I met Mrs. Roosevelt I was interested in her only because she was Theodore Roosevelt's niece. When I was a child, Teddy Roosevelt was THE President, as Franklin Roosevelt would become THE President to a later generation of youngsters.

We met during the Al Smith campaign, in 1928. Her secretary, Malvina Thompson, introduced us. As an Associated Press reporter, the writer was assigned to cover the Democratic National Headquarters, high up in the General Motors building, in mid-town New York. John J. Raskob, who had played a prominent part in the organization of General Motors, was the National Chairman of the Democratic party.

Although the South, then as now, was traditionally Democratic, its population was largely Protestant and strongly opposed to Governor Smith as the presidential candidate because he was a Roman Catholic.

The Associated Press or the AP, as it is generally called in newspaper circles, is made up of member papers, and stories originating in member papers are available for use on the AP wires.

Every now and then during the Smith campaign a story from some Southern member, infuriating to the Democratic national leaders, would slip onto the AP wires. Then the AP reporter at the National Headquarters would have to go to Mr. Raskob and apologize and offer to carry a retraction if he was angry enough. I had been with the AP only a short time, but one day Kent Cooper, the general manager, suggested:

"Why not send that girl over there? At least they won't bounce her out of the twenty-third floor on her head."

They didn't bounce her out on her head, but the expression on John Raskob's face as he saw a woman walk into one of his press conferences the first time was something to remember.

The assignment at National Headquarters was largely routine, except for those occasional apologies to Mr. Raskob. The important job went to experienced political writers, who traveled with the candidate. Once or twice a day Mr. Raskob would hold a press conference, sometimes accompanied by some Democratic bigwig from another part of the country. We got very little news out of them, although some of us found the education of Mr. Raskob, who had never had anything to do with politics before, highly diverting. The real power at Headquarters, Mrs. Belle Moskowitz, Governor Smith's close friend and adviser, seldom saw us, so we really knew little about what was going on behind the scenes.

Sometimes, on particularly dull days, I would wander down to the women's division looking for a feature story. Mrs. Franklin D. Roosevelt was in charge there. I knew little about her, although she had for several years been very active among the women and was better known to politicians around the state than her husband was. But I was rather new to New York, as well as to the AP, and was not familiar with New York state politics.

Her husband, who had run for Vice-President in 1920, the year Harding won, had been crippled with infantile paralysis, had twice nominated Governor Smith for President and was supposed to be one of the party's best orators. In one of those speeches he had called Al Smith "the Happy Warrior," borrowing a phrase from a poem by Wordsworth. The phrase clung to Al all the rest of his life, although there were times when he became a very unhappy warrior. Roosevelt would appear at headquarters occasionally, but we never got much news out of him.

The first person I met in the women's division, was a quiet, self-effacing, businesslike young woman with a determined jaw. She was Mrs. Roosevelt's secretary, Malvina Thompson, whom the Roosevelts—and later nearly everybody else—called "Tommy." We very quickly became friends, for behind her rather forbidding New England exterior there was a great deal of warmth and loyalty and a good sense of humor. Through all the years of our friendship, which lasted until her death, in

1953, Tommy and I never had even a slight misunderstanding or exchanged a cross word.

Tommy, those days, used to refer to Mrs. Roosevelt as "my Boss," and she adored her. Incidentally it was Tommy who later, during the White House years, started calling her "Mrs. R" behind her back, as most of her friends came to do.

I don't remember anything Mrs. Roosevelt said at that first meeting. It must have been brief and formal. She was very plain—she would have used the word "homely"—with prominent front teeth like her Uncle Ted's. She wore her light brown hair tightly tucked under a hair net that even covered part of her forehead. Her clothes were unbecoming. I got the impression that she didn't care much how she looked, so long as she was tidy. She was very tall—almost six feet—and when standing still she looked rather awkward and ungainly. But when she moved, it was with the grace of a fine athlete. Her carriage was magnificent.

A few days later I saw her waiting for an elevator in the General Motors building. Tommy had told me that she was going to debate that day at a women's luncheon with an important Republican woman, a much publicized society matron, who was self-possessed, witty and always beautifully dressed.

Mrs. Roosevelt that day, had she searched the world over, could hardly have found a more unbecoming costume. Waistlines, in 1928, were low, down around the hips. Her black skirt was longer than those worn by most women. She had on a knitted silk kind of jumper, very long, of a shade of green that made her skin look gray. Her hat, set squarely on top of her tightly netted hair, looked like a black straw pancake.

"You poor thing!" I thought. "It will be murder for you at that luncheon."

But I was surprised—and for the first time became interested in Mrs. Roosevelt on her own account—when Tommy told me what had happened. It developed that her opponent had mislaid or forgotten some figures she intended to use. Whereupon Mrs. Roosevelt graciously supplied them for her!

Shortly after that I was assigned to the AP staff covering the Republican State Convention in Syracuse. Theodore Roosevelt's sister, Mrs. Douglas Robinson, was one of the outstanding Republican women in the state. Talking with her, I asked her about her niece, the Mrs. Roosevelt who was a Democrat.

"Eleanor was my brother Ted's favorite niece," Mrs. Robinson replied. "She is more like him than any of his own children."

I used the quotation—she knew she was talking to a reporter, and she hadn't told me not to—but Mrs. Robinson never forgave me for it. I couldn't blame her. She must have had an embarrassing time with her brother Ted's children.

My next memory of Mrs. Roosevelt is seeing her in the noisy, crowded lobby of the Hotel Seneca in Rochester during the Democratic State Convention. She was surrounded by men, the party leaders, and she towered above most of them. They were trying to get her to persuade her husband to run for Governor of New York. She kept shaking her head. In a moment they all entered an elevator headed for a suite on one of the upper floors.

Although the presidential candidate, Governor Smith, wearing his famous brown derby, was drawing huge crowds in the large industrial centers, the party leaders, with their ears to the ground, were worried. They even doubted that he could carry his own state, New York, without a good strong running mate for Governor.

"Frank Roosevelt's my man," Al said. "I've got to have him."

"Frank Roosevelt" was at Warm Springs, Georgia. Daily exercise in the pool there had proved so beneficial that some of his doctors predicted that, if he continued with it for a prolonged period, he might be able to walk again without heavy steel braces on his legs. He had no desire to run for Governor and refused to talk to Governor Smith or any of the party leaders on the telephone. Their only hope was that Mrs. Roosevelt, who had been very active among the Democratic women for several years and was a strong admirer of Governor Smith, might persuade him to change his mind.

None of us reporters, milling around the lobby and the corridors of the Hotel Seneca, knew what was going on at Mrs. Roosevelt's session with Governor Smith and the party leaders. Along toward midnight I saw her go dashing through the lobby and into a cab. She had to catch the midnight train to New York, for she had an early class at the Todhunter School the next morning.

Later we found out that she finally consented to get her husband to the telephone, and when he answered she handed the instrument to Governor Smith and hurried out of the room. As she left, she heard Al's familiar, husky voice saying, "Hello, Frank." Much later she told me that she did not know her husband was going to run for Governor until she read about it in the papers at breakfast the next morning.

She never said whether she wanted him to run or not. She was well aware of the sacrifice it meant for him. The Governor of New York—should he be elected —could not spend weeks at a time in the pool at Warm Springs. But she had said that she never heard him say again, as he had said so often:

"Just you wait and see—I'll be walking again!"

Whatever her feelings were, she kept them to herself. It was his decision to make, and she would not try to influence him.

"A man in public life must make his own decisions," she used to say. "It is the duty of his wife and his family to accept those decisions and cooperate with him in every way possible."

I saw very little of her during the campaign. But on the day after the election I was assigned to get an interview with the wife of the new Governor. Al Smith had lost the election, failing even to carry his own state. But Franklin Roosevelt had been elected Governor by a slim margin.

The interview was in the Roosevelt town house, and, to my amazement, I was escorted up to the drawing room, where a handsome silver tea service was set out. It was most unusual for a reporter calling for an interview with a woman in Mrs. Roosevelt's position to be served tea! It had never happened to me before.

It was a charming experience. I watched with fascination the graceful way she manipulated the tea things with her long, slender hands. She was wearing a lace-trimmed hostess gown, considerably more becoming than the things I had seen her wearing around headquarters. But the hair net was still there, a few strands down below her hairline, on her forehead.

We didn't talk much about politics or the election, but we talked about dogs, after her daughter, Anna, came in followed by her police dog, Chief. I, too, was the owner of a police dog. Curled up at Mrs. Roosevelt's feet was a little black Scotty, named Meggie.

I was given an inventory of the Roosevelt family: Anna, the eldest, blonde and very good looking; Jimmy, a student at Harvard; Elliott, Franklin, Jr. and Johnny, at Groton.

At one point Mrs. Roosevelt said:

"I hope the staff at the Executive Mansion will grow as fond of my children as I know they are of Governor Smith's children."

When we did discuss the election, very briefly, Mrs. Roosevelt seemed much more distressed over Governor Smith's defeat than elated over her husband's victory. She thought the religious issue had had a great deal to do with it, and it made her indignant. But she was reticent and guarded in her remarks, and I felt that she didn't trust me, cordial as she was in her reception of me.

I failed to get much news out of her, but I was so impressed with her graciousness and her charm that I ended my story with this sentence:

"The new mistress of the Executive Mansion in Albany is a very great lady."

The city editor drew a heavy black line through that sentence.

"Too editorial," was his comment.

3

The Governor's Lady

DURING THE YEARS while her husband was Governor of New York, I saw little of Mrs. Roosevelt, although on frequent occasions I covered her husband and came to know him quite well.

I had no reason for trying to see Mrs. Roosevelt. Like many other women reporters those days, struggling to gain a solid footing in their profession, I had a strong aversion to what we called "women's page stuff." I cannot remember ever trying to get another interview with her following that first one, the day after her husband was elected Governor, until after he had won the nomination for President.

Had I tried, I probably should not have succeeded. Mrs. Roosevelt, always gracious, had ways of getting out of being interviewed.

Mary Margaret McBride, in her book *Out of the Air,* recalls one attempt she made. Miss McBride, at that time a successful magazine writer, had an assignment to interview the wives of several important men on how they helped in their husbands' careers. One of the subjects was Mrs. Franklin D. Roosevelt, wife of the Governor of New York.

She met Mrs. Roosevelt on the street one day in New York, introduced herself and asked for the interview.

She says Mrs. Roosevelt smiled, thought a moment, then answered:

"Well, I really think you should see Franklin about that. You'd better come up to Albany. Can you make it next Friday?"

Miss McBride could, was met at the station by Mrs. Roosevelt, was seated next to the Governor at dinner and spent the night at the Executive Mansion.

She got her story. But it must have occurred to her eventually, for she was an experienced reporter, possibly while she was on the train en route back to New York, that she had not interviewed Mrs. Roosevelt at all, but her husband!

While I had no occasion to write stories about her, I wanted very much to know Mrs. Roosevelt. But she always held me at arm's length—and her arms were long.

From Tommy and from Louis Howe, with whom I had become friendly, I heard a good deal about her. Her weekly schedule, as they described it, made me dizzy. On Sunday evenings she would take a train from Albany or from Hyde Park to New York, arriving around midnight. Mondays, Tuesdays and Wednesdays she taught at the Todhunter school. Wednesday evening she would return to Albany and spend the rest of the week fulfilling her duties as hostess at the Executive Mansion.

In addition, she found time to do a good deal of work with the women's division of the Democratic State Committee. For years, until she went to the White House, she raised a modest annual budget for the women's division. As the politicians would say, "the women never had it so good"—before or since. For they did not have to appeal to the men for every cent they spent, as most of the women in both major parties have to do.

Under Louis Howe's supervision—he was a former newspaperman—she edited a small monthly magazine for the women's division. This she continued to do long after she moved to the White House. Many an evening when I was a guest there I saw her go up to her sitting room after dinner—wearing an evening gown—and get out paper, proof sheets, ruler, shears, paste and pencil. With Louis she would make up a dummy of the magazine for the printers.

"Louis will never trust me to write the headlines," she would complain humorously.

Mrs. Roosevelt was good at raising money, much of which, I suspect, she herself contributed. During the early days of the Great Depression—Black Friday, the day the bottom fell out of the stock market, occurred only a few months after her husband became Governor —she raised money with which the Women's Trade Union League, of which she was a member, established in mid-town New York two small, comfortably furnished rooms where women looking for work could go to freshen up, rest, have a cup of tea and a snack. There were little items about them in the papers, but no special display.

The wife of the Governor of New York was also in the furniture business! With three of her friends she started a small furniture factory on the Roosevelt estate at Hyde Park to provide jobs and training for young men out of work. I doubt if they ever made any money out of it. The furniture they turned out was all handmade, beautifully designed and finished—and very expensive. But they didn't go into it to make money, and it served its purpose when it was needed. Later Mrs. Roosevelt had the factory remodeled into a large, rambling house, which she called her "cottage." It became her home, and most of the world's dignitaries—from Nikita Khrushchev to Queen Juliana of the Netherlands—have been guests there.

She was always doing unexpected things. For instance, there was the day in June 1929, when she started for New York from Albany in a little single-motored airplane. Passenger air travel was still rather new at that time. Planes were much smaller than they are today. And slower. There were fewer scheduled flights. Only two years earlier, Charles Lindbergh had flown across the Atlantic, and other pilots were still trying to duplicate his feat and disappearing forever in the fog and mist off the coast of Newfoundland.

It wasn't Mrs. Roosevelt's first flight. She had flown the day before over Albany, Schenectady and Troy, and she had enjoyed the experience so much that she readily accepted when the pilot offered to fly her to New York.

The weather was fair when they took off from the

tiny Albany airport, but presently the pilot found himself heading into a thunderstorm that came rolling up the Hudson River valley, and he set the plane down at Poughkeepsie, where Mrs. Roosevelt caught a train to complete her trip—to the great relief of her husband.

The story did not get much of a play, only a few short paragraphs in the New York papers, but I was greatly impressed with her daring.

Then there was the day in February 1932, when she rode down the Olympic bobsled run at Lake Placid. She only rode part way, the last—and most dangerous—half. It was no child's play. The ice-coated run had some curves that drivers frequently failed to make. Several persons had recently been badly injured on that run, and some had been killed.

Mrs. Roosevelt had gone up to Lake Placid with her husband, who opened the winter Olympic games. When she was asked if she would like to take a ride down the run, she accepted with such alacrity that her husband had no chance to protest. The very idea sent chills up and down my spine, although I was not present and did not see it. But Mrs. Roosevelt?

"Very exhilarating! Wonderful!" was her comment as she rejoined her husband, who had watched the run from a nearby hill.

Later, after I knew her better, I was amazed when she told me that, as a child, she was exceedingly timid. After her Uncle Ted told her to jump off the dock at Oyster Bay, and her mischievous young cousins ducked her, she refused to try to learn to swim and never did learn until she was a grown woman. After her husband became paralyzed, she decided she must learn, so she could teach her two youngest boys, Franklin, Jr., and Johnny. So she took swimming lessons at the YWCA.

During the years Franklin Roosevelt was Governor of New York, I covered him whenever he was in New York City, followed him on several trips around the state and worked as a correspondent on some of his campaigns. Since I was always the only woman in the group of political writers, I came in for a good deal of good-natured ribbing from him. Mrs. Roosevelt says I was the only woman reporter he and Louis Howe knew when Franklin Roosevelt became President. She is probably right, for women covering politics were something of a novelty those days. As a person, I enjoyed him, but I did not take his ideas very seriously. All politicians looked alike to me those days.

Once every summer Governor and Mrs. Roosevelt would take an automobile trip around the state, visiting prisons, hospitals and other institutions. There would be a little procession. First, the Governor and his wife in an open touring car, with the top down. Then one or two cars filled with correspondents.

We never traveled faster than forty miles an hour. That was the speed limit in New York state at that time, and Franklin Roosevelt believed the Governor should obey the law as other citizens were expected to do. A state trooper rode in the front seat beside his chauffeur, Monty Snyder. Sometimes, but not often, there would be a motorcycle escort, but neither the Governor nor his wife liked motorcycle escorts very much. The Governor frowned on the display, and Mrs. Roosevelt was afraid one of the motorcycle men would get hurt.

We'd drive up to some state institution, Mrs. Roosevelt would get out of the car and go inside, and the Governor would invite the superintendent to take a drive around the grounds with him, the correspondents following them. At the end he would usually hold a brief press conference.

If I had been as good a reporter as I fancied myself to be, I'd have followed Mrs. Roosevelt. For I found out later that, under her husband's questioning, she was learning to be a fine reporter herself—acquiring the experience that during the White House years would make her a very special reporter, keeping her husband informed on how the people out around the country were getting along, what they were doing, saying, thinking. She tells a story about one of those visits while she was the wife of the Governor.

"What are the inmates getting to eat?" he asked her as they drove away.

She had copied the menus for the day and showed them to him, but he wasn't satisfied.

"Didn't you look into the pots on the stove?" he demanded.

No public institution in the world ever got a more thorough going-over than Mrs. Roosevelt learned to give the state institutions of New York on those trips. She would pull the covers off beds, examine the mattresses, look into dark corners, open closet doors. It became a lifelong habit with her. To this day a locked closet door presents a challenge to her when she is being shown through the house of a friend! She also learned to watch the expressions on the faces of the inmates and get some idea of their mental attitudes.

But I wasn't there to cover Mrs. Roosevelt. For all I knew, she was merely having a cup of tea with the superintendent's wife. Furthermore, had I tried to follow her, she would probably not have permitted it.

Since we were the only women on those trips, and since I was very much interested in her and wanted to know her better, I used to hope that we might at least be a little bit sociable. But all I could ever get out of her was a very polite "Good morning" or "Isn't it a lovely day?"

I can see her now riding beside her husband in the open car ahead—very erect, wearing a light printed silk summer dress and a hat considerably more becoming than some of those she had worn when I first met her. Someone said her daughter Anna had gone to work on her and had persuaded her to spend a little more money on herself.

But she still wore those hair nets!

4

Convention—1932

In 1930 Franklin D. Roosevelt was reelected Governor of New York by some 800,000 votes, the largest plurality that had ever been given a candidate for the office. Gubernatorial elections were then held every two years.

The depression had grown more and more critical, as plant after plant closed down, and families, with the wage earner out of a job, went through a dreary and frightening routine.

First their savings would go, and life insurance policies would be cashed in or dropped because they could not keep up the payments. The family car, if they had one, would have to be sold—for whatever they could get for it. The market for used cars was glutted. Next it would be their home, usually mortgaged. Finally they would find themselves living in shabby, run-down quarters, with the father selling apples on street corners, hoping to earn enough to buy food.

With Harry Hopkins, a widely known and respected social worker, Governor Roosevelt started a relief program for the unemployed, not unlike the program known as FERA, the Federal Emergency Relief Administration, which they later established in Washington. Obviously the voters in New York approved, for at least something was being done to help them, although it was not enough, and the bread lines were still long, ragged and hungry.

Down by the East River, where the United Nations buildings now stand, men built little shacks out of whatever they could find—old boards, rusty sheets of metal, tin cans pounded out flat. They built bonfires and cooked outdoors. Some people thought they were drunks, consuming wood alcohol. Probably some of them were, but most of them were out of work, unable to get jobs, without even enough money to rent beds in Skid Row. I used to exercise my dog down there, and I talked with some of them. I suspected that the men who worked in the nearby slaughter houses, mostly Mexicans, used to slip them a little meat now and then for their Mulligan stews.

After his impressive victory in his campaign for reelection, it became apparent that the Governor of New York was to be taken seriously as a possible candidate for the Democratic nomination for President.

His chief potential rival was former Governor Alfred E. Smith. But for months neither man would declare himself.

A strange and widening rift had grown up between the two old friends. It began in Albany during the weeks immediately following Roosevelt's first inauguration as Governor. For nearly a month Al remained in Albany, staying in a hotel. Each day he grew more grouchy and morose, the Albany political reporters noted. Finally he returned to New York, gloomy and depressed.

The reporters who knew him thought he had under-estimated Franklin Roosevelt. He probably considered his successor, we reasoned, an amiable, rich young man, who would continue to spend weeks at a time at Warm Springs, leaving Alfred E. Smith to go right on being Governor of New York.

If that is what he thought, he overlooked Roosevelt's Dutch ancestry. Franklin Roosevelt was amiable, but he was ambitious, too—and stubborn. It became more and more apparent that, having been elected Governor, he was going to be Governor. He was setting up his own administration, forming his own policies, making his own plans. He very seldom went to Warm Springs any more.

Al Smith was not in need, materially, although he had probably never saved much out of his salary as a public official. Impeccably honest, he had never accepted any "dirty money." But now some of his friends and admirers stepped in, and he became president of the company that built and owned the Empire State building, with a handsome suite of offices and an income that must have far exceeded anything he had ever earned as a public official.

But it was no life for Al Smith. His whole world had been politics. He had been an elected public official ever since, as a very young man, he had been sent to the State

Assembly from the Lower East Side. He knew little about the world of big business—and undoubtedly cared less. He was becoming a lonely, embittered old man. The warmth of his greeting, when any of us political reporters would drop in to see him, was almost pathetic.

Mrs. Roosevelt took no part in the quarrel between her husband and Al Smith. She and Governor Smith had never been close personal friends, although she admired him greatly for the progressive measures he put through as Governor. She worked hard in his campaigns and once she seconded his nomination when he ran against her cousin, Theodore Roosevelt, Jr. She must have been disillusioned and disappointed when, in the final weeks before the 1932 Democratic National Convention, Al Smith drew closer and closer to the House of Morgan and other big financial interests. But for years—in her sitting room at the White House and later in her home in Hyde Park—there hung on the wall, side by side, framed photographs of Al and his beloved Katie, which they had apparently given her long ago. I used to wonder why she kept them.

Her husband tried his best to repair the breach in the friendship. Once I pointed out to Mrs. Roosevelt two dents in the pavement in front of the Roosevelt town house in New York.

"Those dents," I told her, "were made by my two feet, standing out here with the rest of the gang, waiting for Al Smith to come out and tell us what he and your husband had been talking about."

He never told us—they both had a stock answer: "We were talking about our grandchildren."

The visits were not very frequent—once or twice Al was there for lunch. Usually he would call, staying an hour or so. But he always made it perfectly plain that he was there because Governor Roosevelt had sent for him—that he had not sought the interview. And he did it with a grim kind of relish.

As conditions in the state and the country grew worse, Mrs. Roosevelt took on new activities. Every now and then there would be a paragraph in the papers about her visiting one of the bread lines. And I learned later that she always kept a pot of hot coffee on the back of the stove in her kitchen and material for sandwiches in the refrigerator. When she was approached by some hungry person on the street nearby, she would always send him—or her—to her house, where her cook would serve coffee and thick, nourishing sandwiches. Undoubtedly many of the five-dollar bills, which Louis Howe told me she loved to give away, went to needy persons she met on the street, a boy or a girl hopelessly looking for work.

In the early spring of 1932 I paid my first visit to the Roosevelt home at Hyde Park. Louis Howe arranged for me to go up and take a drive around the place with Governor Roosevelt, who looked more and more like a candidate for President.

A state trooper met me at the railroad station in Poughkeepsie and drove me out to the big, stucco mansion, which belonged to the Governor's mother, but was home to the rest of the family, too.

I was taken into the long library, with a fireplace at either end and a view down the Hudson River. Leaning

over a gate, which bars the entrance, millions of visitors
have looked into that library in the years since the home
was turned over to the government.

We had tea in front of an open fire at the end of the
room farthest away from the entrance. Mrs. Roosevelt
sat on a couch knitting, and there was general conversation, although I don't recall that she said much.

Presently two state troopers carried the Governor out
to his car. He was not wearing his leg braces. It was a
small touring car, with the top down, and it had been
built so that it could be operated entirely by hand.

He drove me down the long, steep hill back of the
house, toward the river and told me how he used to
coast down that hill when he was a boy. Thirteen years
later, Franklin Roosevelt's body would be borne up
that road on a gun caisson to his grave in the rose garden behind a tall hemlock hedge.

At the bottom of the hill, he had what woodsmen call
"a stand of virgin timber," meaning an area where the
trees had never been cut down. He was very proud of it.

"But it's filled with copperheads," he told me. "The
men who go in there to clean up have to wear high boots
and long, thick gloves."

He drove me around the rest of the estate—the farm
and the place where he was raising Christmas trees. He
had bought up some worked-out, abandoned farms and
was renewing the soil by planting little spruces.

"They have to be thinned out every year," he said,
"And those we take out I sell for Christmas trees."

The Governor was an excellent driver, but once we

got stuck in the mud, and a state trooper, following us in another car, had to help us get out.

We were out a long time, for, between them, the Governor and his mother owned some 1,100 acres of land. Their property extended all the way from the river some three or four miles back to the crest of a steep hill, where he later built for himself a cottage, in which he hoped to spend many quiet, peaceful days reading and writing after he retired from the White House.

Finally we drove along a narrow dirt road beside a pond that had been created by damming up a brook, named Val Kill. He called my attention to a little stone cottage on the other side of the pond.

"I built that for my Missis," he said. "I was my own contractor, and the design was mine, although I did have the help of an architect. It's supposed to be a reproduction of a Dutch colonial cottage."

He was immensely proud of the cottage, and, set in beautifully landscaped grounds, it really was lovely.

Mrs. Roosevelt and two of her friends, Miss Nancy Cook and Miss Marion Dickerman, who shared the cottage with her—and spent much more time in it than she could—awaited us there. A short distance back of the cottage was the furniture factory, and the Governor asked his wife to show me through the place.

She was cordial and friendly—in an impersonal way—as she always was. We talked about furniture, but I don't recall anything else she said.

A few weeks later Al Smith finally announced that he would again accept the Democratic nomination for

President if it was offered to him. Roosevelt was by that time an avowed candidate, and the fight was on.

The convention met in Chicago in late June. Louis Howe and, of course, Roosevelt's campaign manager, Jim Farley, were in Chicago. Anna, Jimmy and Franklin, Jr., were there, too. Governor and Mrs. Roosevelt remained in Albany, with two of their sons, Elliott and Johnny.

When on the night of June 30 the convention finally got around to the business of nominating its candidate for President, Roosevelt led the field, with 666¼ ballots. He needed 770, a two-thirds majority, to win. Al Smith had 201 ¾ votes. Jack Garner of Texas, Speaker of the House of Representatives in Congress, was third, a possible compromise candidate, with 90, the votes of Texas and California. Trailing far behind as a remote, but still possible compromise candidate, was Governor Ritchie of Maryland.

The New York delegation was split—65½ for Smith, 28½ for Roosevelt. And the galleries were packed with visitors who hissed and booed the man who had carried the state for Governor by 800,000 votes.

It was an all-night session, unlike anything the Democrats had ever experienced before. There was no endless balloting, like that which had gone on for days in the stifling heat in Madison Square Garden at the Democratic National Convention in 1924. No ballots this time were taken until broad daylight, the next morning. Instead, there were hours and hours of deafening demonstrations and long-winded speeches. There were only three ballots that morning, with Roosevelt and Smith deadlocked. Finally the convention adjourned until evening.

The press associations and the big New York dailies had headquarters set up in the Executive Mansion garage, in Albany. This reporter had been sent up from New York to help Elton Fay of the Albany AP bureau cover the Governor. We had a radio in the garage, telephones and telegraph wires, with operators. But we had little to do, except to listen to the din as it came blaring out over the radio.

The Roosevelts, we were told, were sitting it out in the Governor's study—the Governor, Mrs. Roosevelt, his mother, Elliott and Johnny and two or three close friends. They said Mrs. Roosevelt was knitting—she never sat down those days without her knitting. But around midnight she thoughtfully sent some sandwiches and coffee out to us.

Elton Fay and I were the last to leave the garage that morning, around eight o'clock. Mrs. Roosevelt, looking very clean and crisp in a light summer dress, had just come out on a screened side porch for breakfast. When she saw us come out of the garage, she hurried to the door and invited us in to eat with her. She gave us a good, substantial meal—we were both famished. She had with her a small boy, whom she introduced as Bobby Baker, Louis Howe's grandson.

Impressed as we were by her hospitality and grateful for it, Elton and I were both a little puzzled by her attitude. Not that she wasn't cordial and solicitous for our comfort, but she seemed rather withdrawn—shut up inside herself. She showed little interest in the night's proceedings, appeared unwilling to discuss the subject. That was perhaps natural. But there was something else—something I couldn't define or understand.

"That woman is unhappy about something," I told Elton as we drove away.

"She's probably afraid her husband won't get it," Elton replied. But I wasn't convinced.

Late that afternoon the Governor held a press conference. He appeared fresh, buoyant, confident, laughing and joking with us even more than usual. Naturally we suspected that something was up—what politicians call "a deal." Mrs. Roosevelt sat quietly knitting, her expression serious—almost unhappy. She said nothing.

Our suspicion about a deal was justified. For that evening before they started the next—and fourth—ballot, William Gibbs McAdoo of California walked up to the rostrum and announced that Speaker Garner was turning his ballots—all the votes of Texas and California—over to Roosevelt. They added up to 90 votes. He only needed 12 more to win.

Then the band wagon started rolling, and on that ballot Franklin Roosevelt was nominated. In short order Jack Garner of Texas became his party's candidate for Vice-President.

I was very much surprised, on reading in the files of the New York *Times* the story I wrote that night, to find that I did not even mention the strange look Mrs. Roosevelt had given the girl who asked her if she wasn't thrilled at the idea of living in the White House. It was the only vivid memory I carried away from that press conference—so vivid that it has stayed with me all through the years.

Why I failed to mention it I do not know.

5

Campaign Trail

I BEGAN COVERING Mrs. Roosevelt about a month before the election in 1932.

I did not seek the assignment for myself and did not want it. Interested as I was in Mrs. Roosevelt, I much preferred the job I was doing, covering her husband. But I had felt for some time that Mrs. Roosevelt would be different from other candidates' wives, and that the AP ought to assign someone to cover her.

It wasn't easy to convince the AP. Candidates' wives those days were supposed, like children, to be seen and not heard. They went along on their husbands' trips, but their activities were limited to teas and luncheons in their honor—at which, of course, they did not utter a word for the public to hear. These functions, with the inevitable chicken salad, watercress sandwiches and corsages of orchids, together with a description of what the candidate's wife was wearing, constituted all there was to write about her. The newspapers and the press associations did not consider the assignment rewarding enough to go to the expense of sending someone along to cover her.

The AP finally accepted the idea, however, and Katherine Beebe, the only other woman on the New York news staff, was given the assignment. I took her over to Mrs. Roosevelt's little office at Democratic State Headquarters, introduced them and went happily on my way as one of three AP staff members on the candidate's big campaign swing around the country. Mrs. Roosevelt stayed behind to get Franklin, Jr., and Johnny settled at Groton and did not join us until we were in Arizona on our way home.

The attitude of the crowds made it a fascinating trip. They were large—even at the whistle stops, where the candidate would speak to them briefly from the rear platform of the train. And they were attentive, but usually undemonstrative.

Wherever we went bands played "Happy Days Are Here Again," which had become the Roosevelt campaign song, although it was not his personal selection as many people thought. But the happy days were not here again—not yet. I remember a blistering hot day in Topeka, Kansas, where Franklin Roosevelt, standing on the steps of the state capitol, addressed thousands of deeply tanned, grim-faced farmers, some so ragged that they reminded one of pictures of starving Mongolian peasants in the rotogravure sections of the Sunday papers. They did not cheer. They did not applaud. They just stood there in the broiling sun, silent, listening. No one on

the campaign train that night attempted to do any edu-
cated guessing as to what they had thought of the speech.

Tommy had been sent along to take dictation from
the candidate's advisers, and we saw a good deal of each
other. We ate together frequently in the dining car, and
sometimes late at night, after the last speech had been
made and the last story sent off on the wires, we'd have
long talks, reminiscing about her childhood and mine.
Tommy's people had come from Vermont. They lived
in the Bronx. Her father had been a locomotive engi-
neer, and the New York Central tracks ran so close to
their home that her father would sound three blasts on
the locomotive whistle as his train went roaring by. She
had taught herself shorthand and typing, and the job
with Mrs. Roosevelt was only the third one she had ever
had. She had worked for a time for the American Red
Cross during World War I and had been employed by
the New York State Democratic Committee before she
became Mrs. Roosevelt's secretary.

After Mrs. Roosevelt joined us in Arizona, we went
to Prescott, where our train was pulled off on a siding
to wait for a day while the Roosevelts went out to visit
Mrs. Roosevelt's girlhood friend, Isabella Greenway,
who owned one of the largest cattle ranches in the country. We correspondents were told that it was purely a
social affair, to give the candidate a chance to relax and
rest. There would be no news, and we were not invited.

We accepted the ruling with fairly good grace—although, being reporters, we did not like to let the candidate out of our sight—until we found out that one of our
number had been invited. He was a young man consid-

erably below the professional stature of most of the writers on the train, and he had become friendly with Anna and Jimmy, who were on the trip.

It was probably the worst job in public relations ever inflicted on any candidate. For on that train, cooling their heels on a railroad siding, were some of the most respected and widely read political writers in the country. I wasn't any more important than the young man who had been invited. But I was so indignant that I sought out Mrs. Roosevelt on the train the night before we arrived in Prescott and told her about it.

She seemed more approachable than usual and, to my surprise, she invited me to go along and arranged for my transportation. I decided she must have done it because, as always, I was the only woman among the correspondents, and had covered her husband off and on for the past four years. Tommy was with her, and later she told me that she and Mrs. Roosevelt had had a long talk that night. She didn't tell me what they had talked about, and I didn't ask her.

The story didn't amount to much. I saw some cowboys roping steers and trying to stay on bucking broncos, and I ate some barbecued beef. But Mrs. Roosevelt came and sat with me for quite a long time in the car and told me about her girlhood friendship with Isabella Greenway. Mrs. Greenway had been a bridesmaid at her wedding. After she left me, I departed.

When I got back to the train I found Marvin McIntyre, the candidate's public relations man, raging. He gave me a thorough dressing down, but when he paused for breath, I said:

"Look who's talking!"

I told him we all realized that he probably couldn't help it if some of the Roosevelts invited one of us to go along, when none of us was supposed to go, but I reminded him that Mrs. Roosevelt was a Roosevelt, too, and that she also had the right to invite someone if she chose to do so, and she had invited me.

I then proceeded to share what news I had picked up —which was precious little—with the rest of the correspondents. Mac eventually forgave me, but it must have been a long time before he got back into the good graces of those Washington correspondents—if he ever did.

As we proceeded through Colorado, Kansas, Nebraska, Iowa and into Chicago, I wrote several stories about Mrs. Roosevelt. I wondered about Kay Beebe, but Mrs. Roosevelt said she had seen her only a couple of times. I decided that either she had frozen Kay out, or that the AP had decided that, since I was on the trip, I could cover Mrs. Roosevelt if she did anything worth writing about.

Most of the stories I wrote were about how strenuous she was. I recall puffing, panting and perspiring as I followed her through a cornfield somewhere in Nebraska or Iowa. She moved swiftly, coolly and as easily as though she were accustomed to striding through a cornfield every day of her life. With despair I watched her glide nimbly through a barbed wire fence into an adjacent pasture. When I tried it I got tangled up in the wires, ruined a pair of silk stockings (nylons had not been invented in 1932) and had to be helped.

Although I was not yet aware of the training she had

received from her husband as a reporter while he was Governor, it was perfectly obvious that she was pinch-hitting for him now. We all had lunch with the farmer. Naturally he wanted to show off his farm, and, since it was impossible for her husband, wearing fourteen pounds of steel braces on his paralyzed legs, to walk around the place, his wife did it for him.

We arrived in Chicago in the evening, and Mayor Tony Cermak had the Loop packed with Chicagoans to greet the candidate. There were flaming torches, flares, bombs and brass bands that could barely be heard above the din and the cheering. The crowd broke through the police lines—as they always do—and our cars could barely move as we proceeded toward the lake-front hotel where the Roosevelts were to stay.

There was one awful moment when a mounted cop lost control of his horse, which was apparently frightened by the noise, smoke and lights. The horse reared, and for a split second it looked as though its front hoofs would land in the open car in which the Roosevelts were riding. We correspondents, also in open cars, were a short distance behind. Through the smoke and the flashes of light, I could see Mrs. Roosevelt, sitting perfectly erect, apparently unperturbed!

The following morning, Bobby Fitzmaurice, a member of the Governor's staff who had been taken ill and had had to be left behind, arrived in Chicago to enter a hospital for treatment. Mrs. Roosevelt had had a long and strenuous day, followed by that wild ride through the Chicago Loop, and Bobby's train came in early. She was up in time to arrange for an ambulance to meet him

and accompanied him to the hospital. To my surprise—
I was always surprised when she allowed me to accompany her those days—she took me along.

"Were you frightened when that horse reared over
you last night?" I asked as we rode in a taxi to the station.

"Why, no," she replied, looking a little surprised. "It
all happened so fast that I didn't have time to get frightened."

After a moment's pause, she added:

"If I had been frightened, I'd have been frightened
for Franklin. I can move quickly, but he can't."

I noticed that she always called him "Franklin," never
"the Governor" or "my husband," even to us reporters.

An interesting thing happened that morning. Although thousands and thousands of Chicagoans had seen
her as she rode through the Loop the night before, not
a soul recognized her as we moved about the streets and
the railroad station.

She talked a good deal about Bobby and how fond
she and her husband were of him. But, as always, she
was very reticent about herself, and we did not discuss
the campaign.

The World Series was on in Chicago that day—the
New York Yankees playing the Chicago Cubs. Of course
the candidate and his family had to go to the game. It
would have been considered practically un-American
not to do so. Anyway, Franklin Roosevelt liked baseball.

Mrs. Roosevelt sat between her husband and Jimmy,
squeezed in so tightly that she could not have fallen
over even if she had collapsed. I noticed that her head

had dropped forward, and, on the way out of the ball park, Jimmy told me his mother had slept through the entire game—a World Series ball game, in which Babe Ruth and Lou Gehrig each hit two home runs!

The story I wrote about it got a bigger play than any I had written previously.

6

"She's All Yours Now!"

IN BUFFALO I left the campaign train to help cover the Republican State Convention. When I arrived back in New York, I found that the AP, having decided that Franklin Roosevelt was probably going to be elected, had brought part of the Washington staff up to take over.

I also discovered that Katherine Beebe had resigned and gone off to San Francisco—she had never liked New York. Since I was the only woman left on the news staff —and since it had been my idea in the first place that she be covered—I was assigned to Mrs. Roosevelt.

"She's all yours now, Hickok," Bill Chaplin, the day city editor, said cheerfully. "Have fun!"

I don't know which of us felt more diffident the morning I went over to Mrs. Roosevelt's office and told her of my assignment.

"It means," I said apologetically, "that I shall have

to follow you around all the time, everywhere. I hope I shan't be too much of a nuisance."

Mrs. Roosevelt frowned a little, looked at me commiseratingly, sighed and shook her head.

"I'm afraid," she said, "that you won't have much to write about. I'll not be doing anything very interesting."

Then she added:

"I do realize that it's your job, of course, and you may go with me whenever I do anything publicly."

I decided that she had probably been told by her husband or, more likely, by Louis Howe that it meant a good deal for the AP to assign someone especially to cover her, and that the publicity would help the campaign. No other press association, nor any of the newspapers, had done so. Louis may have talked to her about it—he very likely did—but I found out later that that wasn't the real reason.

That day was her forty-eighth birthday. So, after congratulating her, I undertook to interview her about it. She said only one thing I now remember:

"I'm a middle-aged woman. It's good to be middle-aged. Things don't matter so much. You don't take it so hard when things happen to you that you don't like."

I wanted to ask her what she meant, but I didn't dare. The remark interested me, and I thought a good deal about it afterward. But it didn't make particularly good newspaper copy.

It was along toward the end of the week—she wasn't teaching that morning—and that afternoon she was going to Hyde Park for her birthday party. It would be a small dinner party, the family and one or two close

friends. Naturally I couldn't attend it, so I did not follow her that afternoon.

For days I spent my afternoons—and mornings, too,
when she was not teaching—sitting around outside her
office. Neither Tommy nor Louis Howe could give me
much help.

Jim Farley had succeeded John Raskob as chairman
of the Democratic National Committee, and sometimes
Mrs. Roosevelt and Louis Howe would go across the
street to his office in the Hotel Biltmore. There were
stories going around that Jim and Louis didn't always
see eye to eye about campaign procedure, and I suspected that Mrs. Roosevelt was getting them together
and trying to smooth down their ruffled feathers. But I
could get nothing out of either her or Louis about it.
I might have written what political reporters call a
"dope story," based on speculation. But the AP frowned
on political dope stories. Only solid facts were acceptable. Later I found out that I had guessed correctly, and
what Mrs. Roosevelt accomplished in those meetings
may well have been her most important contribution
to the campaign.

Sometimes she would go out to address small meetings of women. She made no big campaign speeches, did
not speak anywhere outside the state and never mentioned the fact that it was her husband who was running for President.

She was not a good speaker. Her voice, normally soft
and pleasant, would become shrill when she was making
a speech, and she hated making speeches. She also had

a nervous habit of laughing when there wasn't anything to laugh at.

I had reached the point where I was embarrassed whenever I had to go back to the office without any story and expected every day to be called off the assignment, when we took our first trip outside New York City. We went to Syracuse and Binghamton, where she conferred with women leaders and spoke to them at dinners. Still no story that amounted to much.

She seemed a little more friendly, however, and I thought she was beginning to trust me—a little.

At 5:45 on a Saturday morning we arose in Binghamton to catch an early train to Albany. The Governor's limousine was waiting for her at the station, and Monty Snyder, his chauffeur, started off up the hill toward the Capitol faster than he usually drove.

I walked over to the AP office, a short distance from the station, and was struggling with my story when Louis Howe called me from the Executive Mansion. Marguerite LeHand's mother had died at her home in Potsdam, away up on the Canadian border. Miss Le-Hand was Governor Roosevelt's personal secretary. She lived with the family, as did Louis Howe, and everybody called her "Missy."

Mrs. Roosevelt and Missy were leaving within the hour for Boston, where they would spend the evening and catch a midnight train for Potsdam. And—wonder of wonders—Mrs. Roosevelt said I might go along if the AP thought it was necessary!

I tore up the story I had been trying to write, dictated another one over the telephone to New York and asked for instructions.

"Stay with it, kid," Bill Chaplin said after a brief consultation with the day executive editor. "How are you fixed for cash?"

I did not see Mrs. Roosevelt after we boarded the train until we arrived in Boston. She and Missy were in a drawing room. I had a seat outside. We went to a hotel, where they took a suite for the evening. She and Missy dined in the suite, and I went to the AP office and wrote my story. When I went back up to the suite, Missy had retired to the bedroom.

After a moment's hesitation, Mrs. Roosevelt asked me if I would do her a favor.

"Of course," I replied.

"Well, if you can, keep people from bothering Missy. I have a sick friend in a hospital here, and I'd like to go over there."

Shortly after she left, the Boston reporters found us. I told them everything I knew, and I must have convinced them, for they had left when Mrs. Roosevelt returned.

There was only one drawing room available on the train that night, and Mrs. Roosevelt gave that to Missy. She and I found two lower berths in the car outside. Early in the morning the train stopped at a station. I was in the dressing room, and I had noticed, as I passed through the car, that the porter was opening up Mrs. Roosevelt's berth and removing the sheets.

When I had finished dressing and came out, I found Mrs. Roosevelt seated, her berth made up for the day, and set out on Pullman towels on the seat opposite her were cardboard containers filled with coffee and orange juice and some rolls.

She had remembered that there was no diner on the train and had got up in time to get dressed and buy them in the station.

"I thought you'd like some breakfast," she explained.

I did not go to the funeral, but spent the time walking about the town. The funeral procession passed me en route back from the cemetery. Later Mrs. Roosevelt looked me up at the restaurant where I was having lunch. She had borrowed an automobile and asked if I'd like to go for a drive. Our train back to New York would not leave until evening.

We drove along the St. Lawrence River, and she showed me where her husband hoped that some day a power project and a canal, connecting the Atlantic Ocean and the Great Lakes, would be built.

"I don't see so many Democratic posters around," she observed as we drove back through the town. She looked thoughtful and a little sad.

"Franklin is going to be dreadfully disappointed if he loses this election," she said. "For awhile he won't know what to do with himself."

We dined with some of her friends that night. And when we boarded our train, the only space available was one drawing room. All the berths were filled. During the depression, the railroads ran only as many cars as were needed, and they were usually filled.

To my embarrassment, Mrs. Roosevelt insisted on giving me the lower berth and taking for herself the

Mrs. Roosevelt at about the time her husband was elected President in 1932. *Underwood & Underwood, N.Y.*

Mrs. Roosevelt and her secretary, Malvina Thompson, at Democratic National Committee Headquarters in October 1932. *UPI (INS)*

Right: Governor Franklin D. Roosevelt says good-bye to his granddaughter Sistie in front of his house in New York City on his way to Hyde Park. Two days later he was elected President for the first time. *Wide World*

We have only separated by a few
dear Hick & I wonder which
felt worst really!
Eleanor R

"Grief," the Adams Memorial by Saint Gaudens in Rock Creek Cemetery, Washington, D.C., to which Mrs. Roosevelt took the author on a pilgrimage on inauguration eve. *Franklin D. Roosevelt Library.*

Left: Mrs. Roosevelt leaving the White House in January 1933 after visiting Mrs. Hoover. Her inscription to Lorena Hickok reads, "We were only separated by a few yards dear Hick & I wonder which of us felt most oddly! Eleanor Roosevelt." *UPI (INS)*

The President, Mrs. Roosevelt and their eldest son, James, arriving at the White House after the inauguration, March 4, 1933. *UPI (INS)*

Mrs. Roosevelt, second from left, and the author, far right, with
two unidentified friends. *Franklin D. Roosevelt Library*

During a more formal interlude on their visit to Quebec, Canada, July 12, 1933. Mrs. Roosevelt, front row, second from right; the author, back row, second from left. *Edward's, Quebec, Canada*

Mrs. Roosevelt and the author during their trip to the Gaspé Peninsula in July 1933. *Franklin D. Roosevelt Library*

Mrs. Roosevelt with the author in Lowell, Massachusetts, July 1933, during their trip to New England and the Gaspé Peninsula. *Franklin D. Roosevelt Library*

Right: The Roosevelts on the south lawn of their estate at Hyde Park, N.Y., in August 1933. Photographed by Washington newspaperman Robert Armstrong, husband of Bess Furman Armstrong who covered Mrs. Roosevelt for the AP and *The New York Times.* *Franklin D. Roosevelt Library*

Mrs. Roosevelt during her camping trip in Yosemite National Park with the author, July 1934. *Franklin D. Roosevelt Library*

Mrs. Roosevelt, right, with the author and Paul Pearson, Governor of Virgin Islands, in St. Thomas in 1934. *Franklin D. Roosevelt Library*

Above: Mrs. Roosevelt with the author, on her right, during a trip to Puerto Rico in March 1934. *Below:* During their visit to the Caribbean in March 1934, Mrs. Roosevelt with the author, on her left, in long black tie.

Franklin D. Roosevelt Library

On the twentieth anniversary of her first White House press conference, Mrs. Roosevelt gave a luncheon that included the author, front left, in the Algonquin Hotel, New York, on March 3, 1953. *Cosmo Sileo*

long, narrow couch on the other side of the drawing room.

"I'm longer than you are," she said when I protested. "And," she added with a smile, "not quite so broad!"

It was early, neither of us was sleepy, and so we started talking. It was then she told me that I could thank Tommy for the fact that she had accepted me and permitted me to follow her about.

"She's very fond of you," Mrs. Roosevelt said, "and Tommy is a good judge of people. So I decided you must be all right.

"It was hard for me at first. I was brought up by a very strict grandmother, who thought no lady should ever have stories written about her, except in the society columns.

"To be frank with you, I don't like being interviewed. And that applied especially to you. For Franklin used to tease me about you. He'd say: 'You'd better watch out for that Hickok woman. She's smart.' He wasn't criticizing you in any way—he likes you. He was only teasing me."

She then proceeded to tell me about her own unhappy childhood and girlhood, the tragic death of her father, whom she loved so much, her strict Grandmother Hall and her aunts who called her "the ugly duckling."

"May I write some of that?" I asked her fearfully before we finally said good-night.

"If you like," she said softly. "I trust you."

One more story comes to my mind about those days before the election. One afternoon George Akerson, who was handling publicity for the Republican National Committee, with headquarters at the Waldorf-Astoria, asked me to come over and see him. George and I had worked together on the Minneapolis *Tribune,* and we were very good friends. Gleefully that afternoon he took me into his private office and asked:

"Guess who's going to introduce President Hoover at Madison Square Garden tonight?"

I told him I hadn't the remotest idea.

"Mrs. Theodore Roosevelt—I mean Mrs. Theodore Roosevelt, *Senior!*" he told me and grinned at the expression on my face.

I really was stunned. Never in her life before had the widow of Theodore Roosevelt spoken in public or taken any active part in politics. But she had been greatly annoyed right after the Democratic convention in Chicago when she received telegrams congratulating her on the nomination of her "son Franklin." Also there had been a rumor that in Seattle he had tried to have Ted's boys kidnaped to have a picture taken with him. The boys were passing through Seattle on their way to Groton from the Philippines, where their father was high commissioner. The rumor was entirely false, but Theodore Roosevelt's widow believed it. So now she was going to do this thing.

It was a big secret. None of the other reporters had been told. George had tipped me off because he wanted me to be there.

I was. And I shall never forget the murmur that ran through the crowd as Theodore Roosevelt's widow, dressed all in black, walked out on the rostrum and was introduced. She had to be introduced, for she lived in such seclusion at Sagamore Hill that hardly anyone recognized her.

I don't remember what she said—she spoke very briefly. But she made an unforgettably dramatic picture as she stood there before that wildly cheering audience, gesturing with her black-gloved hands. And she got more applause than President Hoover.

I left after she had finished speaking. Mrs. Franklin Roosevelt picked me up in a cab a few blocks from the Garden. I was supposed to go to a meeting with her, but I couldn't. I had to go back to the office and write a story.

"What do you suppose your Aunt Edith did tonight?" I asked as I climbed into the cab.

Mrs. Roosevelt looked surprised and shook her head.

"I can't imagine," she said.

"Well," I told her, "she introduced Herbert Hoover at Madison Square Garden!"

"How very interesting," Eleanor Roosevelt said quietly.

And that was all she said.

7

"Roosevelt Wins!"

THE NEWS APPEARED in big black headlines all
over the country on Wednesday morning, November 9,
1932.

He had won by what the politicians call "a landslide,"
carrying all but six of the forty-eight states, with a total
of 472 electoral votes against 59 for Herbert Hoover.
Nobody was very much surprised, at least nobody among
the correspondents who had been covering the two candidates.

The night before the election Franklin Roosevelt
spoke at a rally in Poughkeepsie, not far from Hyde
Park. That afternoon he had toured his home county as
thoroughly and as conscientiously as though he had been
running for the state senate instead of for President and
had to carry Dutchess county to win!

He spoke late in Poughkeepsie, at 10:45 P.M. It was
well after eleven when he finished.

After the speech Mrs. Roosevelt announced that she was driving down to New York. She would be teaching as usual the next morning at the Todhunter School.

Her husband objected. He did not like to have her drive any long distance alone, especially at night, for she was apt to get drowsy behind the wheel. It was seventy-five miles to New York. It was a rainy night, too, and the blacktop roads—most of the roads were blacktop those days—would be slippery.

"Well, all right," he finally agreed, "if you'll take Hick along to keep you awake."

("Hick" is a nickname I acquired while in college, and it has clung to me ever since.)

We were out in the parking lot when a woman reporter, who had finally been hired by one of the other press associations to cover Mrs. Roosevelt, approached us and asked if she could go along.

"I'm sorry, but there isn't room," Mrs. Roosevelt said.

She was driving a small, dark blue convertible, of which she used to say she owned one third. It belonged to the furniture factory.

"Can't I ride in the rumble seat?" my competitor persisted.

Mrs. Roosevelt shook her head and firmly said, "No." And off we went, leaving the woman standing in the parking lot.

"You aren't going to be able to do that sort of thing after tomorrow," I remarked. "That girl is furious, and I can't say I blame her, even though the AP has spent a lot more time and money having me cover you than her outfit has."

"She'd only get soaked to the skin," Mrs. Roosevelt said calmly. "I couldn't crowd her in here with us. It's not a very good night for driving, and I'll need elbow room.

"And besides, what makes you so sure Franklin is going to be elected?"

"Oh, I have ways of finding out such things," I assured her. "Want to bet?"

She laughed and replied:

"No. But I am by no means so sure he will win as you seem to be."

I thought I detected something almost like a note of hope in her voice!

No woman ever became mistress of the White House with greater misgivings than did Mrs. Franklin D. Roosevelt.

She had three big worries. She talked freely about two of them as we drove through the rain that night. She felt guilty about the third one and never discussed it with me until after the election, although from some remarks she made I had a pretty good idea as to what it was.

First, there was the worry about her husband. A woman as well-informed as she was could hardly rejoice at the prospect of her husband becoming President at that time.

As the campaign drew to a close, conditions around the country had grown worse. Obviously there was no prosperity just around the corner, as President Hoover had hoped. The number of unemployed had increased by millions.

Among them was one large group even more discouraged and embittered than the rest. It consisted of veterans of World War I, who had been promised a government bonus, to be paid at some future time. They wanted it now, while their need was so desperate. During the summer they had staged a march on Washington, had managed to erect rows of little shanties on the Mall, in front of the Lincoln Memorial, and were bringing all the pressure they could on Congress to grant them their bonus immediately.

Their bitterness mounted to fury when General Douglas MacArthur, as Army chief-of-staff, had his soldiers drive them out of Washington and burn their shanties—on orders, it was said, from the White House.

Relief funds in towns and cities were exhausted. Most of the states were running out of money. Organizations like the Salvation Army were having trouble finding enough food for the long lines of hungry people, waiting patiently for a cup of coffee, a doughnut, a roll or, perhaps, a little cup of soup. Something must be done—and quickly. Talk of revolution was in the air.

"Of course Franklin will do his best if he is elected," his wife said that night. "He is strong and resourceful. And he really cares about people.

"The federal government will have to take steps. But will it be enough? *Can* it be enough? The responsibility he may have to take on is something I hate to think about."

Her second worry was about her children—five attractive, high-spirited young people, already somewhat spoiled by their adoring grandmother. She talked to me about their problem that night more than she ever had before. She summed it up this way:

"Of course the public will spoil them at first, and they'll think it's all very exciting and fun if their father is elected President.

"But that same public will turn on them if they make mistakes—as the young are bound to do—and be much harder on them than it would be on other young people."

After a pause she added:

"I know what they'll be up against. I've seen it happen."

I naturally suspected she might be thinking of her Uncle Ted's family. But I didn't ask her.

"They'll have so much to learn," she sighed. "I'll have to keep nagging them, and I hate it. Probably I'm overly conscientious and self-disciplined. But I can't help that. It was drilled into me when I was a child.

"You see the White House won't be really *our* home if we have to move in there. It belongs to the American people. A great deal is expected of families who live there.

"Somehow, if Franklin is elected tomorrow, I'll have to make my children realize that the responsibilities they must take on will far outweigh the privileges they may enjoy. If I have to do it, it isn't going to be easy."

From her somber description of the duties of the wife of a man holding public office in Washington, I had sensed how she felt about her own future, should her husband be elected. The social routine, the calls she had

had to make while her husband was Assistant Secretary of the Navy, the endless teas and the dull formal dinners, the battles for prestige, the petty jealousies—put together, they did not make an attractive picture.

"Aunt Edith did a superb job as White House hostess when Uncle Ted was President," she remarked one day.

She said no more, but the implication was that she did not think she would do so good a job herself if she had to take it on.

Since she had grown to trust me, she left it to my discretion as to whether or not I should quote her. I rarely did during the days before the election. I merely continued to follow her about, describing what she was doing. Newspapers who supported her husband's candidacy would carry some of my stories, but they usually cut them. Newspapers opposed to him threw them into the wastebasket. But still the AP kept me on the assignment and did not appear to be dissatisfied with my output.

I do not remember how I returned to Hyde Park the next day—whether I drove up with her or took the train. She drove up after she had finished conducting her classes in New York and voted in the town hall at Hyde Park. I think I probably went up on a morning train with some of the other correspondents. At any rate, I was in one of the cars in the cavalcade of correspondents who followed the candidate and his wife as they drove down the old Albany Post Road to New York in the late afternoon.

The Roosevelts heard the election returns in a suite at the Hotel Biltmore, where special telephone and telegraph wires and a radio had been installed. The grand ballroom on another floor was jammed with Roosevelt workers and supporters. A big board, on which the returns were flashed as they came in, had been set up there.

Before they went down to the Biltmore, however, the Roosevelts gave a buffet supper at their 65th street town house for their relatives—and there were many of them—their friends and the newspaper people, including the girls who had finally been assigned to cover Mrs. Roosevelt.

She greeted us at the door, and when I came in, she kissed me and said softly:

"It's good to have you around tonight, Hick."

It was the first time I had seen her in evening clothes, and I was amazed at the change in her appearance. The gown she wore was long, with a short train, and it was white, made of some soft material like chiffon. Tall and slender and erect, she looked like a queen in it. I decided that she was as some English women are said to be—they may look rather dowdy in daytime clothes, but in evening clothes they are beautiful.

As the night wore on, the celebration at the Biltmore grew more and more jubilant, noisy and crowded. Even the hotel corridors were filled with celebrants, running back and forth, slapping each other on the back. Well before midnight it was apparent that Roosevelt was elected.

Mrs. Roosevelt was in the suite with her husband and their relatives and some close friends. I hung around outside, but every now and then I would catch a glimpse of her. She was smiling and gracious as she greeted people who went in, but now and then, when she was not talking to anyone, her expression was sober—a little sad, I thought.

In a public room near the suite that night she held her first press conference as prospective mistress of the White House. I thought she had probably not wanted to do it, but the clamor was so great that she finally came out.

She was unusually erect, her head held high. I had learned, from watching her, that she walked that way when she was in trouble or unhappy. One of my most poignant memories is a photograph of her that appeared one morning years later in the New York *Times*, as she followed her husband's casket up the steps into the White House. She was unusually erect that day, her head held high.

Under the hot, glaring klieg lights that had been set up for the newsreel cameramen, she sat surrounded by a mob of reporters and cameramen. It was, literally, a mob. The questions they shouted at her came so fast that she could not possibly have answered them all.

Through it all, she kept smiling, but once she looked directly at me. She shook her head, ever so slightly, and the expression in her eyes was miserable.

I was reminded of a fox, surrounded by a pack of baying hounds—of which, of course, I was one. She was having a bad time, and I knew it. But she carried it off as best she could—and that was good enough.

She said later that one of the correspondents, who had been covering her husband, made his way to her side, leaned over and said in a low tone:

"I wish I knew what you are really thinking and feeling tonight."

She did not answer. She only smiled and shook her head.

I think I could have told him.

8

Just Mrs. Roosevelt?

A FEW DAYS AFTER our train ride to Albany Mrs. Roosevelt held a press conference in the small office she still used at Democratic State Headquarters.

She did it reluctantly, but, now that she was the prospective First Lady of the Land, all the press associations and the New York newspapers had assigned girls to cover her. They kept hanging around outside her office as I had done, alone, when I was first assigned to cover her.

I was not among them, for, since we had become very good friends, I always knew her plans in advance, and we would meet somewhere away from her office.

Knowing what it was like from experience, I felt sorry for my fellow reporters. But the AP, after all the time and money it had permitted me to spend while I was cultivating her as a news source, deserved a break, I thought. And, being a reporter, I liked to get a scoop as well as any of the rest of them did.

Although I don't recall that she said so, Mrs. Roosevelt may have granted their request for a press conference in the hope that, once they'd had one, they would go away and leave her alone. She was somewhat naïve about the press those days.

She was only doing things she had always done. But now everything she did made news. If she took a bus or walked down Madison Avenue alone, that made news. If she was seen standing in the crowd outside a gate in Grand Central station, waiting to board a train to Albany or Hyde Park, that was a story. The wife of a man who would soon become President would be expected to have preferential treatment, but she did not ask for it and did not want it. And—of all the odd behavior in the world—she always rode in day coaches!

Her tweedy suits and white silk blouses were described in the papers. And her hats. Somebody remarked that her hats looked as though she had rushed in and bought them while her bus waited for the traffic light to change. Instead of being offended, she thought it was funny.

She bought apples from men on street corners and carried them in a brown paper bag to her office. Alone, she would go swinging up Park Avenue at dusk, through the crowds.

Women reporters in New York, accustomed to covering Mrs. Hoover, who came up from Washington once a year to attend a Girl Scout dinner, expected Mrs. Roosevelt to have at least one Secret Service man around. But she didn't.

The truth was that she was only trying to be "just

Mrs. Roosevelt." But nobody understood her. And she was criticized because there were so many stories about her in the papers. Some people thought she behaved the way she did to get publicity. Nothing could have been farther from the truth.

The press conference turned out to be something of a disaster. One of the questions asked her was about an inaugural ball.

The idea of an inaugural ball, she told us, seemed inappropriate. With millions of people out of work, ragged and hungry, it did not seem right to her for people who could still afford it to spend all that money on lavish display.

One of the girls misquoted her and wrote that she had said there would be no inaugural ball. As a matter of fact, it was not her decision to make. It would be decided by the Inaugural Committee, made up of Senators and Congressmen and other important Democrats in Washington.

Tommy was present, with notebook and pencil, and her transcribed notes proved that the story was incorrect. Mrs. Roosevelt did not pursue the matter—she did not believe in doing that sort of thing.

Immediately, however, wails of anguish arose from the garment industry, caterers, florists, musicians—every industry and all the unemployed who had hoped to get temporary jobs out of an inaugural ball.

Whereupon Mrs. Roosevelt gave the ball her public blessing and promised to attend it. But the idea was still distasteful to her.

After that, she held no more prearranged press conferences until after she was in Washington, although sometimes she would have to talk to reporters after an event of unusual interest.

Some of the women reporters were more persistent than the rest. One Sunday evening not long after the election, she took an early train down from Albany and came to dine with me, in my apartment. She arrived late and very much annoyed. A girl newly assigned by one of the press associations to compete with me, had hung around Albany all weekend trying to get an interview with her. Of course she got nowhere, for the Executive Mansion was covered by the Secret Service. Under the law, the Secret Service becomes responsible for a man's safety the moment he is elected President. Nobody could get into the Executive Mansion without an invitation. She got none.

Assuming that Mrs. Roosevelt would be going to New York as usual sometime that day, the girl had apparently spent the afternoon in the Albany railroad station, and, when she saw Mrs. Roosevelt go through and board a train to New York, she followed her. Fortunately—from Mrs. Roosevelt's standpoint—the train was crowded, and the girl could not find a seat anywhere near her.

She caught up with her, however, in Grand Central station, and the conversation that followed, as repeated to me by Mrs. Roosevelt, went something like this.

Girl reporter: "Where are you going, Mrs. Roosevelt?"

Mrs. Roosevelt: "I'm dining with a friend."

Girl reporter: "Who is your friend?"

Mrs. Roosevelt: "I'm sorry, but I cannot tell you. It's a purely private and personal engagement."

Girl reporter: "May I follow you and wait outside?"

Mrs. Roosevelt, emphatically: "You may not! I told you it's a private, personal dinner engagement. There will be no story about it."

Girl reporter: "But I *have* to follow you, Mrs. Roosevelt."

Mrs. Roosevelt, beginning to get really annoyed: "I'm sorry, but you *cannot* follow me. If you insist, I shall spend the rest of the evening right here in the station. But I am *not* going to be followed—by you or by anybody else."

The girl finally gave up and left, and Mrs. Roosevelt took a cab to my apartment.

"Why didn't you tell her where you were going?" I asked. "It might have satisfied her, and she'd have left you alone."

"I was afraid it might embarrass you," Mrs. Roosevelt replied with a sigh.

The second time she got into trouble was over a remark she made on the radio. It may have been the first time she ever spoke over the radio. It could have been an interview, but it was probably a speech, for radio interviews were not common those days.

She undertook to explain why she thought the prohibition amendment would have to be repealed. Because of personal tragedies in her family, Mrs. Roosevelt did not drink herself and was strongly opposed to drinking. She once told me that the very smell of alcoholic beverages was distasteful to her. But the prohibition amendment had not really worked. The bootleggers, organized under men like "Scarface Al" Capone, were the first racketeers this country had known. And the law was so widely disregarded that it had become a joke.

"Nowadays," Mrs. Roosevelt said, "a girl who goes out with a boy must know how to handle her gin."

She had made the remark in irony, but a large section of the public did not take it that way, and she was roundly abused. Even some of the newspapers which had supported her husband and had been friendly toward her carried editorials criticizing her.

There are some pleasant and humorous memories of those days between Franklin Roosevelt's election and his inauguration as President. Times, for instance, when I was invited to the Roosevelt town house for meals. The President-elect was never there for a meal when I was. When he was in the house, it was filled with his advisers, coming and going, as he went about the job of selecting his Cabinet and laying out his program.

The first invitation I received was for Sunday night supper. The dining room in the 65th street house was on the ground floor. The kitchen was in the basement, and the food was hauled up on a dumb-waiter and served by Reynolds, the Roosevelt butler.

We were served scrambled eggs, with little sausages. They were delicious, and I was hungry, so, when I was offered a second serving, I took it. Reynolds removed the plates, and next, to my surprise, on came cold sliced chicken and roast beef and a salad! This was followed by a very tasty dessert. I left the table feeling like a Strasbourg goose!

Later I learned that the Roosevelts always had scrambled eggs, cold meat, salad and dessert for Sunday night supper. At the White House and usually, I believe, when her husband was present, Mrs. Roosevelt scrambled the eggs herself, at the table in a chafing dish—possibly because he liked to watch her do it.

Then there was the time when I met Franklin Roosevelt's "Aunt Kassie." I was invited to lunch and next to me at the table was an elderly woman, whom Mrs. Roosevelt introduced as Mrs. Collier.

As we started lunch, Mrs. Collier explained that she was Franklin Roosevelt's aunt, his mother's sister. I later learned that the family called her "Aunt Kassie." Mrs. Collier was very much perturbed over the amount of publicity her nephew's wife was getting. And there I sat, chief perpetrator of the crime!

I remarked mildly that it was very difficult for a person in Mrs. Roosevelt's position to avoid publicity.

"Nonsense!" Mrs. Collier said most emphatically. *"I have never talked to a newspaper reporter in my life!"*

I nearly choked over my soup and spent the rest of the meal in mortal terror lest, in the general conversation, it might come out that I was a reporter.

Mrs. Roosevelt said her husband roared with laughter when she told him about it, and for some time thereafter, on the rare occasions when I saw him, he would ask:

"Have you seen my Aunt Kassie again? Has she found out about you?"

Once he said:

"You should have answered her: 'Well, you're talking

to one now!' She could have taken it. She has a sense of humor."

But I'd as soon have tried to stroke a man-eating Bengal tiger!

One morning I was having breakfast with Mrs. Roosevelt when Georgiana, her cook, came rushing up from the kitchen in terror. Franklin Roosevelt had a valet named McDuffie, a very likable individual. The family and all of us who knew him were fond of him. But every now and then McDuffie would have too much to drink.

"McDuffie's down there, and he's been drinking!" Georgiana panted. "He and Reynolds are having a fight, and Reynolds is going after him with a carving knife!"

Mrs. Roosevelt arose from the table and went down to the kitchen, followed by her trembling cook. A few minutes later she returned, sat down and went on with her breakfast.

"Well, what did you do with them?" I asked.

"I took the knife away from Reynolds and sent McDuffie to bed," she replied calmly.

There was one luncheon I intended to give, but Mrs. Roosevelt wouldn't let me. Since I was attached to the New York bureau of the AP, I knew I'd not be covering Mrs. Roosevelt any more after she moved to Washington. Bess Furman was on the Washington staff, and I suggested that the AP have her come up to New York, so that I could introduce her to Mrs. Roosevelt.

She came one day in the late winter. I had intended to take them both to lunch. (It would have been a perfectly legitimate item on my expense account.) But Mrs.

Roosevelt insisted that I take Bess up to the 65th street house for lunch. The President-elect was away that day.

I did not know Bess very well—I don't believe I had ever met her. But whenever I had a story on the wires that she liked, Bess used to write me a warm, friendly note about it. I thought it was very generous of her.

The luncheon was a success. Mrs. Roosevelt liked Bess, who was an unpretentious, friendly person, and Bess liked her. They became great friends.

One evening toward the end of January I went up to Mrs. Roosevelt's house to go out to dinner and the theater with her. The following week she was going down to Warm Springs, to help her husband celebrate his fiftieth birthday. She planned to stop in Washington en route to look over the White House, as incoming First Ladies do. Families living in the White House usually, I believe, partly furnish their private living quarters themselves. At least, the Roosevelts did.

With an amused expression on her face, she handed me a telegram to read. It was from Mrs. Hoover's secretary, addressed to Mrs. Roosevelt's secretary.

Mrs. Hoover's secretary wanted to know where Mrs. Roosevelt would like to have a White House car pick her up in Washington. And would she like to have her military aide in uniform or in civilian clothes?

Since Tommy had left when the telegram arrived, Mrs. Roosevelt had answered it herself, over Tommy's name.

Her wire stated that Mrs. Roosevelt would not need a White House car, and that, under no circumstances, did she want a military aide—in uniform or out.

We both laughed, and then I asked her:

"But how are you going to get there if you don't go in a White House car?"

"Why, I'll walk, of course," she replied, looking surprised. "I'll go down on a midnight train, have breakfast at the Mayflower Hotel and walk over. It's only a short distance."

"May I go along?" I asked.

She looked amused and a little puzzled as she replied:

"Of course, if you want to. But I really don't see how you're going to get much of a story out of *that*."

9

One Day in Washington

A FEW NIGHTS LATER Mrs. Roosevelt, Elliott, Louis Howe and I took a midnight train to Washington.

We arrived early in the morning, and Mrs. Roosevelt raced down the long platform and through the station as though she were fleeing for her life.

Louis and Elliott were some distance behind us, both laughing—probably at me. When she walked at her normal speed, it was hard for me to keep up with her. That morning she left me fifteen paces in the rear!

I think she was afraid she might find a White House car waiting for her at the curb, but there was none. She leaped into a cab, I fell in after her, and we were off. Elliott and Louis did not accompany us.

At the Mayflower we were taken to the presidential suite. I was impressed, but Mrs. Roosevelt was annoyed. She thought one room would have served her purpose. I don't know how many rooms there were in the presidential suite—I didn't count them—but we certainly were not crowded.

While we were at breakfast, which we had sent up, Mrs. Roosevelt looked thoughtful and said:

"I think this would be a good time for me to meet Mrs. Garner. I've never met her."

She left the table and went to the telephone, calling back over her shoulder:

"Do you know where the Garners live?"

I said I thought they lived at the Hotel Washington. She proceeded to look up the number in the telephone book and gave it to the Mayflower operator. A moment later I heard her say:

"I'd like to speak to Mrs. Garner if you please."

Since Jack Garner was not only Speaker of the House, but would presently become Vice-President of the United States, the switchboard at the Hotel Washington was not putting calls through to the Garner apartment unless they were acceptable.

"This is Mrs. Roosevelt," I heard her say. There was a pause.

"Mrs. Franklin Roosevelt," she said. Another pause. Then patiently:

"Mrs. Roosevelt. R-o-o-s. . . . ."

At that point, the Mayflower operator apparently cut in, and I heard:

"Mrs. Garner, this is Eleanor Roosevelt. How are you?"

Mrs. Garner, undoubtedly somewhat surprised, apparently said she was feeling fine and asked Mrs. Roosevelt how she was.

"Oh, I'm always well," Mrs. Roosevelt said. Then she added:

"I have to go over to the White House for a little while this morning, and, if you are going to be at home, I thought I might drop by to see you."

Apparently Mrs. Garner thought she should be the one to pay the call. So they agreed to meet at the Mayflower that afternoon.

Shortly after ten o'clock that morning, Franklin Roosevelt's cousin, Warren Delano Robbins, chief of protocol in the State Department, arrived with his wife. Mr. Robbins was the son of Roosevelt's "Aunt Kassie," by her first marriage.

Since Mrs. Roosevelt had declined Mrs. Hoover's offer of a White House limousine, Mr. and Mrs. Robbins had come to get her and take her to the White House in a State Department car. Mr. Robbins was horrified when she announced that she was going to walk over.

"But Eleanor, darling, you can't do that!" he protested. "People will recognize you! You'll be mobbed!"

"Oh, yes, I can," Mrs. Roosevelt said firmly. "Miss Hickok is walking over with me."

She had introduced me without telling them that I was a reporter, but I felt that they viewed me with some distaste.

They stayed and argued with her for some time, to no avail, and they finally left and drove sadly away in the State Department car.

Mrs. Roosevelt had been right—it was only a short distance to the White House. We walked a couple of blocks down Connecticut Avenue, through a small park, along Jackson Place, past the house where Stephen Decatur had once lived, and crossed Pennsylvania Avenue to the northwest gate to the White House grounds. She did not race, as she had through the railroad station, but she walked faster than she usually did, and, as always, I had trouble keeping up with her. She was recognized only once, by a smiling little old lady, who wished her good luck.

I had been in Washington only once before—and then not as a reporter. I didn't know that reporters were admitted to the White House grounds, so I waited for Mrs. Roosevelt at the gate. I saw several persons standing around in front of the stately white columns at the entrance, but I didn't realize that they were reporters. The only newspaper people I knew in Washington were the political writers I had met on the campaign train and they were not around that morning.

Mrs. Roosevelt, walking unusually erect, her head held high, passed quickly through the group and went inside. I think she was there about an hour, but it seemed much longer to me, as I stood waiting at the northwest gate.

Finally she came out, paused for a moment while a photographer took her picture and came racing down the long, curving driveway. Several of the people who had been standing outside the entrance started to follow her—and only then did I realize that they were reporters. But she was too fast for them, and they gave up the chase. They did not know that I was a reporter, too.

As we walked back to the Mayflower, she told me that Mrs. Hoover had been very gracious, had shown her

through part of the house and had then turned her over
to Ike Hoover, the head usher, who had been there
since the days of William McKinley. Ike, who had
known her when she was a girl, visiting her Uncle Ted,
had greeted her as "Miss Eleanor."

"I think it was sweet of him," she remarked. "It made
the whole experience seem a little less stiff and formal."

She would have to talk to her husband, she said, before she made any final decisions.

"But the oval room on the second floor, which Uncle
Ted's family used as a sitting room, would make a good
study for Franklin," she remarked. "There's a room and
bath right next to it.

"There's a big room next, which President and Mrs.
Hoover apparently use as a bedroom. I'd like to make
that my sitting room, and next to it is a bathroom and
a small dressing room, which I may use as my bedroom.

"Mrs. Hoover has a conservatory, with a lot of plants
in it, at the west end of the hall, but I think I may have
those removed, put up screens and make it into a family
sitting room. The hall is very wide."

Mrs. Hoover, she said, had gathered together some
pieces of beautiful old furniture which President Monroe had presented to the White House and had placed
it in a small sitting room near the rooms the Roosevelt
boys would use when they were at the White House. Ike
Hoover had told her they called it the "Monroe Room."

"I hate to do it," Mrs. Roosevelt said, "but I shall
have to move it out and distribute it in safer places
around the house. Can you imagine what would hap-

pen to that lovely furniture if my boys ever started roughhousing in there?"

I left her at the Mayflower, took a cab to the AP office, wrote my story and joined her, Elliott and Louis for a late lunch at a little old hotel up near the Capitol. Louis had an aversion to the big, plush downtown hotels like the Mayflower.

During lunch there was some discussion as to what Mrs. Roosevelt would do if she was in a crowd with her husband and somebody started shooting at him.

"I'd step in front of him, of course," she replied promptly. Wearing his leg braces, Franklin Roosevelt moved slowly and awkwardly.

"That would be just dandy," Elliott observed. "Then you'd both get shot."

"Oh, but I have a weapon," Mrs. Roosevelt said.

She hauled out of her handbag an object that looked like an oversized fountain pen.

"You press this little thing here, and it shoots out tear gas," she explained earnestly, pointing it straight at Elliott, who ducked.

Louis, Elliott and I were so convulsed with laughter that none of us could speak for a moment. When he finally caught his breath, Elliott said:

"Can't you just picture the scene? The guns will be blazing away at Pa, and Mummy will be fishing things out of her handbag, throwing them right and left, saying: 'It's here—I *know* it's here. I saw it only this morning.' While Pa will be saying patiently: 'You'd better hurry, dear!'"

We all thought it was very funny, but I had noticed

during the campaign, while her husband was making a speech, Mrs. Roosevelt would keep turning her head this way and that, as if she were looking for something. She was, she told me later, looking for fire exits.

"If a fire had broken out in one of those places, and the crowd started to panic," she said, "it would have been almost impossible to get Franklin out. Without his leg braces, two men can pick him up and carry him easily and quickly. But when he is wearing his leg braces, he is so awkward and unwieldy! He can't move himself or be moved quickly."

I met her later that afternoon, just before she and Elliott took off in a small plane for Warm Springs, and she told me about her talk with Mrs. Garner. They had liked each other immediately. Mrs. Garner was a plain, down-to-earth sort of woman. For years she had been her husband's secretary and cooked his lunch on an electric grill in his office.

At one point in the conversation Mrs. Garner said anxiously:

Mrs. Roosevelt, do you think I can go on being Jack's secretary?"

"I most certainly do!" Mrs. Roosevelt replied. And I could imagine the feeling with which she said it.

Later Mrs. Garner said:

"I really don't know much about Washington society."

The Garners had never gone out in formal society, and it was said that Jack Garner had not even owned a dinner jacket—let alone white tie and tails—until he became Speaker of the House.

"If you see me making any mistakes, Mrs. Roosevelt, will you please tell me?" Mrs. Garner asked hesitantly.

"Of course," Mrs. Roosevelt assured her. And she added:

"If you see *me* making any mistakes, will you please tell me?"

I knew she must have said it very sincerely—and very gently.

I wanted to write a story about it, but Mrs. Roosevelt asked me not to.

"I wouldn't mind," she said, "but Mrs. Garner might not like it."

Mrs. Roosevelt returned to New York from Warm Springs a few days after her husband's birthday, and we continued to see a great deal of each other.

One night in February we dined in an Armenian restaurant, of which I was very fond. Later that evening we were taking a train to Ithaca, where Mrs. Roosevelt was to speak the next day on the Cornell ·University Farm-and-Home Week program. Her husband had been on a fishing trip aboard Vincent Astor's yacht the *Nourmahal,* and he was due in Miami that night.

The restaurant was fairly well downtown. On our way uptown we stopped somewhere in the West Forties, and she made a brief speech to some motion picture executives and received a large bouquet of red roses. We took a cab, she dropped me at the AP office and went on up to her house. We planned to meet later in Grand Central station.

As I walked into the AP office the night city editor shouted at me:

"Where's Mrs. Roosevelt?"

"On her way home in a cab," I said. "I just left her."

"Get the hell up there quick!" he ordered, still shouting. "Some crackpot in Miami just tried to shoot her husband!"

10

"One Cannot Live in Fear"

MRS. ROOSEVELT AND LOUIS HOWE were in her husband's room when I arrived. They had heard the news—probably from the AP, for I had hastily scribbled down the Roosevelts' covered number before I dashed out of the office.

Reynolds had let me in, quickly closing the door behind me. But there was no one around outside except one policeman, who was there every evening. Having seen me going in and out with Mrs. Roosevelt, he recognized me and didn't challenge me.

Louis was at the telephone, frantically trying to get a call through to Miami. He kept jiggling the receiver up and down and yelling "Operator!" as people do when they try to put through a long-distance call in a hurry and get no results.

Mrs. Roosevelt was sitting on the foot of her husband's bed. She was very pale. Her face looked drawn, her expression strained. But she only said, quietly:

"This is what it's like to be in public life, Hick."

Finally, in despair, Louis slammed down the receiver, and the moment he did so the telephone started to ring.

It was Franklin Roosevelt, calling from Miami to tell his wife he had not been hit and was all right. As Louis handed her the telephone, her husband asked her to pass the word along to his mother.

He had left the *Nourmahal*, and on his way to the station to entrain for New York he had been asked to drive through a park, where a large crowd waited to greet him. He had made a short impromptu speech and was about to drive on when he saw Mayor Tony Cermak of Chicago emerge from the crowd. He had ordered Monty Snyder to stop, and he and Tony shook hands and exchanged a few words.

Tony had started to move away, toward the back of the car, when somebody in the crowd started shooting. Tony was hit. He had taken Tony into his car and had held him in his arms as they drove to the hospital. Tony was unconscious, and his shirt front was soaked with blood. He had felt for Tony's pulse, couldn't find it and thought he must be dead. But Tony had regained consciousness by the time they reached the hospital.

He said Tony was now up in the operating room and he intended to stay right there at the hospital until the doctors could give him a report. He thought some woman had been hit, and one bullet had grazed the hand of a Miami police detective who was standing by the car.

He hadn't been able to see much, because Gus Gennerich, his bodyguard, whom he was planning to take to Washington with him, had slammed him down on the seat in his open touring car the instant the shooting started and had sat on him! His ribs felt a little sore, he said. Gus was no lightweight.

I left as soon as Mrs. Roosevelt had finished talking with her husband. She had a number of calls to make, to her mother-in-law and other members of the family. Her husband had also asked her to call Jim Farley and tell him he would not be in New York in time for their appointment the next day.

Reporters began arriving at the Roosevelt house a few minutes after I left, she told me when we were aboard the train, and there was a lot of confusion, but she had finally managed to get away. There must have been considerable confusion, for one of the New York papers the following morning had Mrs. Roosevelt leaving for Ithaca "accompanied by her maid." I was her "maid."

We didn't talk much. I remember only one remark she made, after telling me about the confusion.

"That drive to the hospital must have been awfully hard on Franklin," she said. "He hates the sight of blood."

Reporters began coming around as soon as we arrived in Ithaca. She was calm and relaxed as she talked. I discovered that day that the Roosevelts bounced back quickly after a near-tragedy. Of course the news about Tony Cermak that morning was good. The doctors predicted he would recover, although he did die later. One of the bullets had hit a woman, but she was not seriously hurt. And one bullet had hit the rear of her husband's car!

Referring to the attempt on her husband's life, she said quietly:

"That's apt to happen to any man in public life. He must always face the possibility, and so must his family. But it's best not to think about it any more than you have to."

She looked thoughtful for a moment and added:

"One cannot live in fear."

Later that morning her husband telephoned her from Miami. He had left the hospital late, after the doctors had assured him that Tony was going to be all right, had spent the rest of the night aboard the *Nourmahal* and was leaving shortly for New York, where he would arrive the next morning.

He thought he had better ask the Secret Service to send a man up to protect her. Under the law, members of the family of a President or a President-elect were covered by the Secret Service only if he requested it. Mrs. Roosevelt was indignant.

"Don't you dare do such a thing!" I heard her say. "If any Secret Service man shows up in New York and starts following me around, I'll send him right straight back where he came from."

There was a pause, while her husband apparently told her he was really concerned for her safety and thought it best to take no chances.

"I know, darling," she replied. "But nobody's going to try to shoot me. I'm not that important."

After another pause, I heard her say, teasingly:

"You have to have them around, poor dear, and I'm *so* sorry for you!"

Then she added:

"But I don't have to—and I won't! I'm not going to have any Secret Service man following me around. *I simply will not have it!"*

The curbs were lined with uniformed policemen, standing almost shoulder-to-shoulder as Franklin Roosevelt drove from the railroad station to his home on his arrival in New York. But Mrs. Roosevelt told me later that, after he had entered the house, he grinned, waved a hand in the direction of a hotel across the street and said:

"All those policemen out there couldn't have prevented it if anybody had really had a mind to shoot me. Anybody could have rented a room in that hotel, sneaked a rifle up to his room and taken a pot shot at me out the window as I was getting out of the car! I'd have made a perfectly beautiful target."

As inauguration day grew closer and closer, Mrs. Roosevelt talked to me a good deal about her dread of what lay ahead for her as mistress of the White House. How much she talked to her other friends about it I do not know. But except to her husband and Louis, I doubt if she said very much. Her friends—even some of her most intimate friends—were so thrilled and happy over her husband's election that they would have found her attitude difficult to understand.

As she saw it, she would be a pallid, ineffectual copy of her Aunt Edith, who had been one of the most successful and admired hostesses the White House had ever had. Mrs. Coolidge had been good at it, too, although Mrs. Roosevelt wondered if she had really enjoyed it.

"Of course, her years there were overshadowed by a terrible grief," she remarked one day.

She was referring to the loss of Calvin Coolidge, Jr., a young boy, who blistered his foot while playing tennis on the White House court. The blister broke open, infection set in, and he died of blood poisoning. Today, his life could have been saved. But there were no "wonder drugs" back in the 1920s.

Mrs. Roosevelt thought she would be a kind of prisoner—behind gilded bars. Her activities, she expected, would be severely limited, although she intended to keep on editing *Babies—Just Babies,* for which she thought she would be harshly criticized.

"But I can't help that," she would say. "I'll just have to go on being myself, as much as I can. I'm just not the sort of person who would be any good at that job. I dare say I shall be criticized, whatever I do."

Her husband, when he had time to talk to her—his days were crowded with conferences, a stream of idea-men and job-seekers following him wherever he went —and Louis Howe tried to reassure her. They kept telling her it wasn't going to be the way she thought it was going to be. But she wouldn't believe them.

Being followed about by reporters was bad enough. But the thing she hated most was having her picture taken. And the photographs of her in the newspapers were anything but flattering.

Somebody told her she must not look glum and sour-faced when she was being photographed. She must smile. So smile she did. Usually it was a kind of set smile. Sometimes it was uncertain, sometimes wistful. But smiling only accentuated her prominent front teeth.

I once remarked that it was too bad that the cameras did not capture the warmth and charm of her personality. She shrugged her shoulders and said:

"My dear, if you haven't any chin and your front teeth stick out, it's going to show on a camera plate."

The women in her mother's family, the Halls, had all been noted for their beauty. Mrs. Roosevelt, too, had a beautifully shaped nose and brow, and her eyes were lovely. I decided that the upper part of her face was Hall, and the lower part Roosevelt. Unfortunately her "Roosevelt mouth" was much more prominent in pictures than her Hall nose, brow and eyes.

Drearily she went about the business of ordering her inauguration gown. The fittings bored her. She selected a light blue material, with a slight touch of gray in it. The papers, of course, all carried descriptions of it. It did not turn out to be a particularly becoming dress, although the color did bring out the blue in her eyes. Harking back to the days when Alice Roosevelt's favorite color was "Alice Blue," the papers called it "Eleanor Blue."

Later, after she moved to Washington, a top-flight Fifth Avenue designer began making her clothes, and during the White House years Mrs. Roosevelt was always beautifully dressed. Her evening gowns were magnificent. No other woman I ever knew could wear

a low-back evening gown as well as she could—or handle
a long train.

Every year—usually in June—the Roosevelts used to
give a party for the press in the East Room of the White
House. The President—without his leg braces—would
sit in an arm chair, laughing and joking with the correspondents. At some time during the evening, the
Marine Band would play a waltz. Mrs. Roosevelt did not
know the modern dances, but she did know how to
waltz. She would flip her long train over her arm and
waltz with her brother, Hall, who was even taller than
she was. They both waltzed beautifully, and everybody
else would leave the dance floor to watch them. They
made an unforgettable picture.

All through January and February and right up until March 2, the day they left for Washington, Mrs.
Roosevelt continued to do the things she had always
done. The papers continued to carry stories about her.
And some people continued to criticize her. They just
couldn't get used to the idea of her being "plain, ordinary Mrs. Roosevelt." Some of them hoped that, once
she was in the White House, she would mend her ways.
And very unhappily, Mrs. Roosevelt thought so, too.
She thought she'd have to do it.

She used to end every discussion of her future with
the remark:

"Well, anyway, I'll get caught up with my reading.
I'll have plenty of time on my hands."

For women who held jobs and made their own way in
the world she had an admiration and respect that
amounted to almost awe. Once she said to me bitterly:

"If I really had to go out and earn my own living, entirely on my own, I'd have to do it as a scrubwoman. And I'd probably not be very good at that. I have no profession—no training for anything."

I reminded her that she was a teacher.

"Don't forget," she said, "I have a financial interest in that school."

She had some sad last duties to perform. She gave up the little office she had had all through the years while she worked as a volunteer at Democratic State Headquarters. She gave her desk to Tommy and her chair—a very beautiful walnut chair that had been made at her furniture factory—to me.

She could no longer go about the state, she thought, conferring with the women leaders. Nor could she continue to raise the women's division budget. But she decided to keep on editing the women's division magazine. Compared with a McFadden publication, it was an innocuous little magazine.

I did not ask to go with her the day she taught her last classes at the Todhunter School. I thought she would rather not have any outsider around.

The last night before the Roosevelts went to Washington, she came to have dinner with me in my apartment. Her husband, as usual, was tied up in conferences with his advisers. So she ordered dinner for them and left.

She referred to that evening as her last night out of captivity.

11

Inauguration Eve

IN THE LATE AFTERNOON of March 2, 1933, the Roosevelts left for Washington and the inauguration.

They went down from New York on a special train, with members of their family, Louis Howe, some of Franklin Roosevelt's "Brain Trust," as the newspapermen called it, a number of Secret Service men and the reporters.

Although I'd not be covering Mrs. Roosevelt any more —on her arrival in Washington she would become Bess Furman's responsibility—I, too, was aboard that train. For a very special reason.

Arrangements had been made for me to interview Mrs. Roosevelt immediately upon her arrival at the White House following the inauguration. To get that interview, I had obtained not only her permission, but that of her husband, and I had volunteered to let Louis Howe read the story before I turned it in. It was supposed to be the first time the wife of a President was ever interviewed by a newspaper reporter in the White House. It would be the last newspaper story I'd ever write about Mrs. Roosevelt.

Just before we arrived in Washington I saw Mrs. Roosevelt for a few seconds. I had taken charge of her Scotty, Meggie, on the way down so she wouldn't be in the way back in the private car. As I turned Meggie over to her, she said:

"If you can pick me up at the Mayflower early tomorrow morning—a little before eight—there's something I'd like to show you. It's something that used to mean a very great deal to me when we were in Washington before."

She told me to meet her with a cab at a side entrance to the Mayflower that opened into a little foyer off the main lobby. From that foyer there was an elevator that went up to the presidential suite and to some large and expensive apartments.

"There will be Secret Service men there," she said, "but I'll tell them you're coming, and I'll try to be just inside the door when you drive up. I don't want to be followed, and that early in the morning I don't think we shall be."

My cab had hardly stopped the next morning when she slipped out the entrance and climbed quickly in beside me. She told the driver to take us out along R street, in Northwest Washington.

"I'll show you the house where we used to live," she said.

But as we approached the place, she caught sight of a

large sign on the lawn: "Former Residence of Franklin D. Roosevelt." Hurriedly she told the driver to move on and directed him to take us to a cemetery—Rock Creek Cemetery.

It was a fairly long drive, and we made it mostly in silence. She seemed wrapped up in her own thoughts—and memories.

Upon our arrival at the cemetery, she directed the driver, without any hesitation, through a maze of winding driveways—she had obviously been there many times before—until we came to a clump of small trees or shrubs, evergreens of some kind, through which I could see a large bronze statue.

We left the cab, walked around in front of the statue and sat down on a curved stone bench, facing it. For some moments she sat gazing at the statue in silence.

The bronze figure, considerably larger than life-size, was that of a woman, seated, her body enveloped in the folds of a robe that extended up over her head, like a cowl. Only her face was visible. It was a face that no one who had seen it could ever forget.

It was a beautiful face, a strong face. But the beauty and the strength were not in the features—the wonderful contours of the mouth, the nose, the almost closed eyes. The beauty and the strength were in the expression.

As I looked at it I felt that all the sorrow humanity had ever had to endure was expressed in that face. I could almost feel the hot, stinging unshed tears behind the lowered eyelids. Yet in that expression there was something almost triumphant. There was a woman who had experienced every kind of pain, every kind of suffering known to mankind and had come out of it serene —and compassionate. Whatever bitter unhappiness, whatever agony of body or soul the viewer might be going through that woman had known. She would understand.

Finally Mrs. Roosevelt spoke, in a hushed tone, as though she were in church.

"It's by Saint Gaudens," she said. "He called it 'Grief,' but it's better known as the Adams Memorial. Henry Adams had it erected here, in memory of his wife."

After a long pause, she spoke again, slowly, almost as though she were talking to herself:

"In the old days, when we lived here, I was much younger and not so very wise. Sometimes I'd be very unhappy and sorry for myself. When I was feeling that way, if I could manage it, I'd come out here, alone, and sit and look at that woman. And I'd always come away somehow feeling better. And stronger. I've been here many, many times."

During the drive back to the Mayflower she told me she had known Henry Adams, descendant of the distinguished Adams family of Massachusetts and author of one of the most widely read autobiographies in this country during the years immediately after World War I, *The Education of Henry Adams.*

"He used to drive up to our house in a carriage," she said. "But he didn't come to see me. He came to see my children. I'd send them out, he'd invite them into the carriage with him, and he'd sit there and visit with them

—sometimes for a long time. The children loved him, and he was apparently fond of them."

After I had dropped Mrs. Roosevelt off at the Mayflower, I went down to the AP office. Byron Price, chief of the Washington bureau, invited me into his office. His expression was skeptical as we faced each other across his desk, and he asked:

"Is Mrs. Roosevelt really the natural, unaffected person your stories make her out to be?"

"I think so," I told him. "If I'm wrong, Bess Furman will find out."

Years later, when he was Assistant Secretary General of the United Nations, and Mrs. Roosevelt was a delegate from the United States and chairman of the Commission on Human Rights, I used to wonder sometimes if he still felt skeptical about her. But I think he must have lost his skepticism long before her husband died and she moved out of the White House.

Washington was in a turmoil that day, but not because of the impending inauguration. Grandstands had been erected along Pennsylvania Avenue, of course, buildings were decorated with red, white and blue bunting, and crowds were pouring into the city.

The turmoil, however, was due to something far more significant. During the past few days the country had reached the lowest ebb in the Great Depression. There were runs on the banks, and one after another they closed, frantic depositors pounding on the doors, demanding their money. The clamor of a desperate, frightened public rose louder and louder. People who lived through those days must remember how they felt. Anything could have happened. Only a spark was needed to set it off!

That afternoon the President-elect and his wife called on President and Mrs. Hoover, following a custom that had existed in the past. Mrs. Roosevelt told me later that President Hoover had wanted her husband to join him in issuing a proclamation closing all the banks in the country temporarily. But Franklin Roosevelt refused to accept any responsibility until he was in office.

"I think it made Mr. Hoover pretty unhappy," she said. "Although Mrs. Hoover was as gracious as could be, President Hoover treated Franklin with coldness. He was even a little rude to him."

I was in my hotel room, thinking about going out to dinner, when Mrs. Roosevelt telephoned.

"Franklin is tied up," she said. "There's a continuous stream of people coming and going—his sitting room is right next to mine. Jimmy and Louis are with him. The other children are all out, and I'm alone. Would you mind coming over and dining with me?"

The big lobby of the Mayflower was swarming with newspapermen that evening, eagerly grabbing any little crumb of information that came down from the presidential suite. But they were barred by the Secret Service men from the side entrance. Mrs. Roosevelt had phoned down that she was expecting me, and I slipped through unnoticed.

We had dinner sent up, but neither of us felt much like eating. As the evening wore on, we kept moving restlessly about, pacing the floor. Every now and then

Jimmy or Louis would come in with the latest reports from around the country. They were all bad.

"Anything could happen," Mrs. Roosevelt kept saying with a worried frown. "How much can people take without blowing up?"

Late in the evening her husband sent in the final draft of his inaugural address for her to read before it went to the mimeographers. She read it aloud to me.

"It's a good speech, a courageous speech," she said after she had finished. "It has hope in it. But will the people accept it? Will they believe in him?"

We tried to map out the interview I was to have with her the following day—the reactions to watch for in the crowd. I'd not be up at the Capitol to hear the inaugural address. I'd be waiting for her at the White House. But we got nowhere. The story just didn't seem very important, not even to me.

I could have had my own private worry that evening, but it would have seemed ludicrous, compared with Mrs. Roosevelt's worry. It was her husband who was going to have to bring hope into the hearts of a frightened, desperate people. It was her husband who tomorrow must face a huge audience from the East Portico of the Capitol. It would be the first time he had faced a big crowd since the night in Miami, when a man tried to kill him. It must have occurred to her, as it did to me, but she never would have mentioned it. Her concern was as great—if not greater—for the people. Under the circumstances, it was impossible for me to think about my own private worry, and I didn't. Not that night.

Nevertheless, there I was, a newspaper reporter, right

in the middle of what, that night, was the biggest story in the world. And I did nothing about it.

It did not even occur to me at the time, but I could have slipped out to a telephone after she read the inaugural address to me and could have given the AP the gist of it, with a few quotations. And I could have told about the reports coming in from around the country to the room next door. I knew who was there, who was coming and going. If I had, it would have been a scoop—the biggest scoop of my career. But scoops and my career did not seem important that night, even to me.

My suffering, my sense of guilt came later. One day I talked about it to Louis Howe. But he did not give me any comfort.

"A reporter," he commented drily, "should never get too close to the news source."

I never discussed it with anyone else. But while I did not realize it at the time and remained with the AP several months longer, that night Lorena Hickok ceased to be a newspaper reporter.

It was very late, around three or four in the morning —nobody kept track of the time that night—when Jimmy came in, looking half dead with fatigue, dropped into an armchair, sighed and announced:

"They've all left. Pa's going to bed."

Mrs. Roosevelt went in to say good-night to her husband. After she left I slipped off my dress and shoes, put on the dressing gown she had handed me and lay down on one of the twin beds in her room. I must have been asleep when she returned. But tired as I was, it was not a restful sleep. I had a recurring dream that comes back to me almost as vividly now as it did that night.

In my dream I saw thousands of people—a crowd extending all the way back from the Capitol to the House office building and the Library of Congress. They stood there, silent, listening. In their silence there was something almost menacing. And beyond them I could dimly make out some pillars against the background of a massive building and a platform where a man stood, alone, talking to them.

12

"A Little Terrifying"

MRS. ROOSEVELT'S SITTING ROOM, on the second floor of the White House, with two large windows facing out across the South grounds to the Washington Monument, looked as cold and gray as the weather outside when I was ushered into it in the late forenoon of March 4, 1933.

The day before had been sunny and mild, but a raw, damp wind blew down Connecticut Avenue, and heavy clouds darkened the sky when we took Meggie for a short walk early that morning.

As we parted at the side entrance to the Mayflower, Mrs. Roosevelt told me she had asked Ike Hoover, the head usher at the White House, to take me to her sitting room, where I was to wait for her during the ceremonies at the Capitol.

"Don't look so worried," she said with a smile that was both amused and a little sad. "Nobody over there is going to bite you."

But I was nervous and jumpy as I walked slowly up the long curving driveway to the impressive white columns and the polished glass door, where Ike Hoover met me. It was the first time I entered the White House.

The big room, with its lofty ceiling and tall windows, had the depressing look of a room that had just been vacated. Not that it was empty. An enormous and very ugly mahogany bed had been moved in and made up, with a plain white counterpane. It looked like makeshift furniture, and it was. I found out later that it had been brought in that morning from the government warehouse. There were chairs about, a big sofa near the fireplace.

Along one side of the room two enormous mahogany wardrobes frowned down at me. These, I learned later, after Mrs. Roosevelt had transformed the place into a bright and cheerful sitting room, had to stay there. For the White House had practically no closets.

But in spite of the furniture, the place looked empty. There were square and oblong marks on the gray walls, where pictures had hung. It was completely impersonal —no books or magazines about, no little knicknacks such as people have around when they live in a place.

One of the radiators was leaking a little, and now and then it made a thumping noise, followed by a hissing sound. The room not only looked cold—it *was* cold.

Before we parted that morning Mrs. Roosevelt had handed me a little card, admitting me to a small Episcopal church across Lafayette Park from the White

House. Her husband would attend a service there before going up to the Capitol for his inauguration.

"Since you won't be up at the Capitol," she said, "I think you might like to attend the service."

The church was so small that there was room only for the Roosevelt family, a few relatives and close friends, the incoming Cabinet and a limited number of correspondents.

The service was brief and simple. Franklin Roosevelt's favorite hymn, "Eternal Father, Strong to Save," was sung. The Reverend Endicott Peabody, still "the Rector" at Groton School, as he had been when Franklin Roosevelt was a boy there, prayed to Almighty God to grant to "Thy son, Franklin" strength and wisdom to meet the heavy tasks that lay ahead of him.

After it was over, I stood in the crowd in Lafayette Park and watched two long, black automobiles move through the northwest gate and up the driveway to the White House. The first one was a touring car, with the top down, and on the rear seat a man wearing a silk hat sat alone—the incoming President of the United States. It was followed by a limousine, in which Mrs. Roosevelt too was riding alone.

The grandstands that had been erected along Pennsylvania Avenue for the parade obscured our view of the entrance. But a few moments later, the two cars emerged through the northeast gate, out into Pennsylvania Avenue. There were now two men on the rear seat of the open car, the incoming President had been joined by his predecessor. And in the limousine Mrs. Hoover rode with Mrs. Roosevelt.

Motorcycle cops raced their motors, and the two cars, followed closely by a Secret Service car, with men riding on the running boards, headed past the Treasury building and turned the corner, around which they would swing back into Pennsylvania Avenue and on up to the Capitol.

A few minutes after I arrived in Mrs. Roosevelt's sitting room, Ike Hoover came in, carrying a small silver tray on which there was a tall glass of orange juice. It was a gracious thing for him to do—he could have sent a servant. But I'm afraid it wasn't properly appreciated. I already felt chilled to the bone, and, if there is anything colder than a tall glass of orange juice when you're already shivering, I don't know what it could be!

After I had dutifully drunk the orange juice, I started moving about, trying to get warm. One of the first things I noticed was a silver plate, riveted into the brick facing around the fireplace. On it was engraved an inscription, stating that this had been Abraham Lincoln's bedroom when he lived in the White House! Later I often slept in that room, on a very comfortable Val Kill daybed, which Mrs. Roosevelt had put in for any intimate friend who might be visiting her when the rest of the house was full—as it usually was. And sometimes, just before I went to sleep, I would think of a careworn, troubled President pacing up and down in that room far into the night.

I stepped to the door and peeked out into the west end of the hall, where Mrs. Roosevelt had said Mrs. Hoover had her conservatory. She apparently had some giant ferns, bigger than any I had ever seen before, with very long prongs. In the dim, gloomy light, I was reminded of pictures I'd seen of a prehistoric forest. I half expected to see a dinosaur come strolling out!

I looked about for a radio, but there was none. I had thought I might be able to tune in the ceremonies going on up at the Capitol. Finally I went over and stood by one of the windows, waiting. And wondering.

After what seemed like hours, I heard motorcycles and cheers. President and Mrs. Roosevelt were about to arrive at the White House.

They drove in through the South grounds to an entrance under the South veranda that led into a floor below that which is usually described as the first floor of the White House. During all the years he lived there, President Roosevelt always used that entrance, for there were no steps, up or down.

Even so it was a long walk for a man with paralyzed legs held rigid in heavy steel braces—through a large room and down a wide corridor to the elevator. Since he could not use his legs, he had learned to swing himself forward, using the muscles of his hips and his back. With the support of a cane and the strong arm of one of his sons or a Secret Service man, he could walk—slowly and awkwardly and with what must have been agonizing effort.

The President, Mrs. Roosevelt and Jimmy were in the open touring car. All three were smiling, and I felt a great surge of relief, although there was a lump in my throat, as several Secret Service men hurried forward to help the President out of the car.

But Mrs. Roosevelt was not smiling when she came into her sitting room. Her expression was sober as she walked over and stood by one of the windows, drawing off her gloves.

"It was very, very solemn," she said slowly, "and a little terrifying.

"The crowds were so tremendous, and you felt that they would do *anything*—if only someone would tell them *what* to do!"

She stared somberly out the window for a moment, then added:

"I felt that particularly because, when Franklin got to that part of his speech in which he said it might become necessary for him to assume powers ordinarily granted to a President only in wartime, he received his biggest demonstration."

I did not notice it at the time, nor do I think it occurred to her, but in her discussion of the crowd's reaction to her husband's inaugural address, Mrs. Roosevelt never mentioned the famous line—the only sentence out of that speech that will never be forgotten: "The only thing we have to fear is fear itself."

Jimmy—later Congressman James Roosevelt of California—says quite some time elapsed before it was taken up and widely quoted. It got little attention in the newspaper accounts the following day.

Neither of us spoke for a moment, and I was wondering—but did not ask her—if she was thinking the same thing I was thinking. The people wanted a leader, and, in their desperation, they could have chosen the wrong kind of leader.

Americans who gave it any thought at all at that time were concerned about Huey Long, "the Louisiana Kingfish." But thanks to Franklin Roosevelt and the New Deal, Huey Long's one-man rule never extended far beyond the borders of his own state. In another land, however, that seemed very far away those days, the German people—who in the years following World War I had suffered even more than we had in our Great Depression—wanted a leader, too. They accepted a man whom nobody had taken very seriously before, a funny-looking little man with a Charlie Chaplin mustache and a lock of hair plastered down over his forehead. On January 30, 1933, Adolf Hitler became Chancellor of the German Reich.

At this point we were both a little startled to see one of the White House servants, who walked as noiselessly as cats, standing in the doorway. He wanted some instructions, which Mrs. Roosevelt gave him. Then she continued:

"No woman entering the White House, if she accepts the fact that it belongs to the people and therefore must be representative of whatever conditions people are facing, can lightheartedly take up her residence here at this time."

That was a quotation, to be used in my story. She might have added, as she looked at me and shook her head, misery in her eyes:

"Least of all, *this* woman."

We tried to go on with the interview, but we were interrupted so many times by members of her family and the staff that we finally retired to her bathroom to finish it.

"What I wanted to say," she began again, "is that one

has a feeling of going it blindly. We are in a tremendous stream, and none of us knows where we are going to land.

"The important thing, it seems to me, is our attitude toward whatever may happen. It must be willingness to accept and share with others whatever may come and to meet the future courageously, with a cheerful spirit."

Most of the rest of the interview consisted of things she had told me before. Much of it I had already written. She repeated a statement she had made to me many times—her determination to simplify White House social affairs.

"Neither Franklin nor I would want to do anything that would detract from its dignity, which we both love," she said. "But I believe things could be made a good deal simpler without that."

She would, she said, try to greet her guests at the door herself and see them to the door when they left. The usual procedure called for the guests—self-conscious and ill-at-ease—to be assembled in the Red Room or the East Room depending on the size and formality of the party. Finally one of the ushers or a military aide would appear in the doorway and announce in sepulchral tones: "Mrs. Roosevelt." That was the way it had been done in her Aunt Edith's day.

"Do you think you can get away with changing it?" I asked.

"Some people probably won't like it," she acknowledged. "I shall probably be criticized. I expect that."

As we said good-by, she told me she hoped to get up to New York for a brief visit very soon.

"Perhaps in a week or ten days," she said hopefully.

Although the AP thought well enough of my story to copyright it, it got lost in the shuffle of big news that day. So many things happened—big things, important things. There was the President's speech, to which columns and columns were devoted, the speech itself, editorials and comments about it.

In the Oval Room on the second floor of the White House which became his study, the new President had his Cabinet sworn in that afternoon by a New Yorker, elderly, scholarly Associate Justice Benjamin Cardozo, of the Supreme Court. President Roosevelt greatly admired Justice Cardozo, both as a jurist and as a man. Never before had a President had his Cabinet sworn in on inauguration day. And this Cabinet included for the first time a woman. Miss Frances Perkins became Secretary of Labor.

Up in New York Governor Herbert Lehman had ordered all the banks closed the previous Friday, and it was expected that the new President would take the same drastic action on a nationwide scale, which he did a couple of days later.

But while my story did not get much of a play—it appeared on page seven of the New York *Times*—another AP story out of Washington made page one in many papers all over the country. It was a lively, colorful story—undoubtedly written by Bess Furman—about what Mrs. Roosevelt did that day, not what she said or thought.

It started with this sentence:

"The century-old White House wore a startled air today as its new mistress took over."

She had expected 1,000 guests for tea, but 3,000 came. Tea was served not only in the state dining room, but in the East Room as well. Nothing so startling had happened to the sacrosanct East Room since Abigail Adams had hung her wash there to dry! And even the press had been invited to tea!

The new First Lady had been interviewed in the White House by a newspaper reporter. Nothing like that had ever happened before. She had had seventy-five guests for dinner and had come downstairs to greet them at the door.

The story ended with this observation:

"Washington has never seen the likes of Eleanor Roosevelt!"

13

Getting Settled

IN THE LATE EVENING of Monday, March 6, Mrs. Roosevelt telephoned me from the White House to tell me about her first press conference. I had returned to New York on Sunday.

I was anxious to hear how the conference had gone, for I knew she had been reluctant about adopting the idea, even though her husband and Louis Howe had encouraged her to do it. She probably would not have done it at all, had she not been convinced that for the wife of the President to hold press conferences for women reporters only might help some of them to keep their jobs.

"I was a little nervous at first," she admitted, "but the girls were so nice and so friendly that I got over it quickly.

"We had it in the Red Room. Thirty-five came, and of course there weren't enough chairs, so some of them had to sit on the floor, but they didn't seem to mind. I

don't think they got much news out of it, but they
appeared to be satisfied.

"It really wasn't bad. I think I'll continue with them."
She laughed and added:

"I really beat Franklin. He isn't holding his first press
conference until Wednesday!"

I had already read about the press conference in the
afternoon papers. Mrs. Roosevelt had come into the
Red Room carrying a large box of candied fruit, which
she passed around. The conference had not produced
much news, but apparently everybody had had a good
time, including Mrs. Roosevelt.

Some of the editors were skeptical at first and predicted that Mrs. Roosevelt's press conferences would not
continue longer than six months. But they continued all
the years she was in the White House. She held her last
one on the morning of April 12, 1945. That afternoon
the President died in his cottage, "the Little White
House," in Warm Springs, Georgia.

To the end she stuck to her original plan—only women
reporters were admitted. Again and again men tried to
get in, using all kinds of ruses, to no avail. Only one
man made it. And he was the King of England!

In the early spring of 1939, several months before
King George VI and Queen Elizabeth visited this
country, Jimmy Roosevelt was in London and was
invited to Buckingham Palace. Upon his return home,
he told his mother that the Queen had expressed great
interest in her press conferences and had wondered if
it would be possible for her to attend one, as an observer.

After some display of reluctance on the part of the

people who surround kings and queens and tell them what they may or may not do, it was decided that, although she could not, with propriety, actually attend Mrs. Roosevelt's press conference, she could appear at the close, and that the women reporters could be presented to her. That press conference took place on June 9, while the King and Queen were guests at the White House.

As it had been arranged, the women reporters lined up in the hall outside the Red Room at the close of the press conference. The Queen appeared and started down the line, Mrs. Roosevelt presenting each of the reporters to her.

They had gone only a few steps when everyone looked startled. The Queen glanced around—and looked startled, too, and a little dismayed. For following closely behind her was her husband, the King, with a mischievous, boyish grin on his face. He had slipped in unnoticed, while everyone was watching the Queen—the only man ever to get into one of Mrs. Roosevelt's White House press conferences.

On the day she left the White House, Mrs. Roosevelt invited the women who had attended her press conferences to come and say good-by. She also invited the men who had covered her husband, and some of them came over from the press room in the executive wing of the White House. But that was not a press conference. They only came to say good-by.

Mrs. Roosevelt's White House press conferences did not always produce what reporters call "live news." Some of them were routine. But no city editor dared ignore them, for sometimes she would appear with a highly newsworthy guest.

One day in August 1942, it was Queen Wilhelmina of the Netherlands, who, after Mrs. Roosevelt had introduced her, took over the press conference and ran it herself. It was the first time a reigning monarch had ever held a press conference in Washington, and it was the first time the Queen had ever held one.

One thing those press conferences did for Mrs. Roosevelt. She came to know and like reporters. And they liked her. With one or two exceptions, I have never known any newspaper person, man or woman, who did not like Mrs. Roosevelt. Very few people in public life have had press relations as good as hers have been all through the years.

Before her husband's first term as President had ended, Mrs. Roosevelt herself became a newspaper writer, with her daily column. Some editors were also skeptical about how long that would last, but she continued writing it three days a week, for more than a quarter of a century. When she started writing her column, she promptly joined the Newspaper Guild, the reporters' union.

Once, in the autumn of 1936, Mrs. Roosevelt was seriously ill with a virus—in all the years I knew her, I can recall only three times when she was sick in bed. Her husband offered to write her column for her, but she turned him down and dictated it to Tommy—while she had a temperature well above 100 degrees.

"I was afraid that, if I let him write it, he'd take it

over, and I'd lose my job," she explained jokingly
afterward.

Before we said good-by on the telephone that night,
three days after she had moved into the White House,
she told me she had been very busy getting settled. There
wasn't a bed in the White House long enough for the
President, except the huge mahogany bed in which
Abraham Lincoln was supposed to have slept and two
big four-posters in the large guest rooms.

"Any one of them would make his little bedroom
much too crowded," she said. "I'm having a bed made
for him up at Val Kill. I'm making progress, and I think
you'll see quite a few changes when you come down."

As she went busily about her job of getting settled,
Mrs. Roosevelt, I learned later from Tommy, frequently
filled the White House staff with dismay. She was only
being herself, but they weren't used to her yet.

The big, old-fashioned, slow-moving White House
elevator was of the self-service type. It was customary,
however, for one of the ushers to escort the First Lady
from her sitting room to the elevator and operate it
for her. As they stepped in, he would push a button
that rang a bell, announcing that she was aboard. The
first time Mrs. Roosevelt wanted to go downstairs, however, no bell rang. She stepped into the elevator,
operated it herself and walked into the ushers' office
before anyone knew she had left her sitting room. After
several futile attempts, the staff gave up and let her run
the elevator to suit herself.

Helplessly—and very uncomfortably—the well-trained
servants stood by as she moved furniture around herself

until she had it placed where she wanted it. They tried
to help, but she was too fast for them.

She wanted the telephone in her sitting room moved
and could not understand why it hadn't been done. She
sent Tommy to find out. Tommy came back grinning.

"The poor man," she announced, "has been sitting
out there in the hall for hours, waiting for you to get
out. He didn't dare come in while you were here."

"Oh, spinach!" said Mrs. Roosevelt, using one of her
favorite expressions. "Tell him to come on in and get
started!"

Late in March I was invited to a dinner given in honor
of Mrs. Roosevelt in Washington by the Women's
National Press Club. I was Bess Furman's guest at the
dinner and I spent the night at the White House. I
remember that visit very clearly because of a lesson I
learned—the hard way.

The dinner was given at the Hotel Willard, and Mrs.
Roosevelt and I picked up Mrs. Garner on our way. At
the Willard I followed them into the elevator. When it
stopped, I was nearest the door, so I did what seemed
the logical thing to do. I started to step out.

But suddenly the long arm of a Secret Service man
shot out in front of me, and I was unceremoniously
pushed back! Thus did I learn that nobody except the
President is supposed to precede the First Lady through
a doorway. The expression on my face must have been
funny, for when I looked around at Mrs. Roosevelt and
Mrs. Garner they were laughing. As a matter of fact, I
hardly ever had to stop and remember that bit of
etiquette, for the simple reason that I nearly always

followed Mrs. Roosevelt anyway. I couldn't keep up with her.

She had been right when she told me on the telephone that I would notice some changes. Mrs. Hoover's conservatory had been moved out, big screens had been set up, and the end of the hall had been converted into a family sitting room. Always, while the Roosevelts lived there, it was called the West Hall sitting room. Furniture that looked as though it had been bought during the Grant administration had been moved in from the government warehouse—a sofa and chairs, all covered with red plush and decorated with ball fringe!

"But I'm having slip covers made for it," Mrs. Roosevelt said, "nice, bright, cheerful material."

Backed up against the screens was a big, walnut dropleaf table, from her furniture factory. All the years she lived in the White House, Mrs. Roosevelt had breakfast served in the West Hall sitting room, except in the summer, when she liked to have breakfast out on the South veranda. The Roosevelts loved to eat outdoors. Close to the house, right under one of Mrs. Roosevelt's sitting-room windows, there was a huge old magnolia tree, which Andrew Jackson had planted when he lived in the White House. Frequently in warm weather Mrs. Roosevelt had tea served out under that tree, and sometimes lunch.

The most noticeable change was in her sitting room— a very characteristic change. I've always said I'd know the minute I walked into a room if Mrs. Roosevelt lived there—because of the number of pictures in it. One great big wall in her sitting room was covered with pictures—mostly photographs in plain black frames. There wasn't an inch to spare! And there were pictures on the other walls, too, wherever there was space for them.

In her duplex apartment in New York, according to the man who hung them for her, she had more than two hundred pictures. And she must have had at least that number—probably more—in her house in Hyde Park. Mostly they were photographs—her family, her friends, and celebrities from all over the world. She also had some beautiful paintings, which were wedding gifts to her and her husband.

In her effort to make life in the White House a little less formal Mrs. Roosevelt was aided and abetted by her husband. He was no stickler for protocol either. Because he was obliged to move slowly, it annoyed him when people hung back, waiting for him to precede them. Many times I've seen him impatiently wave them ahead.

Mrs. Roosevelt tells a story about her husband's attitude toward White House etiquette. When you are with the President, you are not supposed to leave the room until he does, or until you are dismissed. One Sunday soon after they moved in, the President and Mrs. Roosevelt had a few guests for tea in the Oval Room, which had become his study. The party was intimate and informal, and the President was enjoying himself thoroughly.

Among the guests were Mr. and Mrs. William H. Woodin. Mr. Woodin was President Roosevelt's first Secretary of the Treasury. He died after about a year in office and was succeeded by Henry Morgenthau, Jr., who held the post until after President Roosevelt's death.

It began to get late, and the Woodins had another engagement. Finally Mrs. Woodin whispered to Mrs. Roosevelt, explaining that she and her husband had to leave and asking that the President excuse them.

"Darling, the Woodins have to leave," Mrs. Roosevelt said.

"Well, why don't they?" the President asked, arching his eyebrows in surprise.

One of the things a new President has to put up with is the change in attitude of people toward him. Franklin Roosevelt, a friendly, gregarious soul, found it trying. He used to complain humorously about the ladies seated on either side of him at luncheon or dinner.

For a time he kept a score on the number of "Yes, Mr. President" and "No, Mr. President" he got as he tried to engage them in conversation.

"That's all I can get out of them," he would say. "They just won't talk to me.

"Being President is a lonely job. When people do talk to me, they tell me what they think I want to hear—or ought to hear. Or they want something."

The truth is that most Americans hold the President in such awe that they are apt to become speechless in his presence. I was no exception.

Sometime in May 1933, I was invited to the White House for a weekend. I arrived on a late evening train, and Mrs. Roosevelt met me at the station in her new convertible with the top down. It was painted "Eleanor blue," the color of the gown she wore to her husband's inauguration.

We drove to the White House, and, after she had shown me the new slip covers in the West Hall sitting room and other changes she had made, we took Major, her police dog, and little black Meggie for a walk around the South Grounds.

As we arrived back in her sitting room she said;

"Now you must go in and say good-night to Franklin."

I hung back. I had not seen him on my visit in March. This would be our first meeting since he had become President.

"What on earth is the matter with you?" Mrs. Roosevelt asked.

"I'm afraid of him," I confessed—in a very small voice.

"Why, Hick," Mrs. Roosevelt said, "you've known him longer than you've known me. He hasn't changed. He's still the same man."

Reluctantly I followed her into the Oval Room. He greeted me cordially, of course. He always treated me as any gentleman would be expected to treat a friend of his wife. Besides—he and I had been friends before I knew Mrs. Roosevelt very well.

"What were you afraid of?" Mrs. Roosevelt asked when we returned to her sitting room.

"Well—he's the President," I said lamely. "I just can't help it."

My feeling never changed, even though I saw a good deal of him during those early White House years. He used to tease me unmercifully at times and we had some gay, enchanting visits.

But to the very end, he was always "Mr. President" to me.

And Mrs. Roosevelt remained "Mrs. Roosevelt." In the early days just before and just after she moved to the White House, she used to try to get me to call her "Eleanor." But I couldn't do it.

"My dear," I protested one day, "I can't go around bawling 'Eleanor' to the wife of the President of the United States!"

That was something I should not have said. It was cruel, for it only reminded her of her altered status, about which she was already unhappy enough.

"It's damned inconvenient when the husband of one of your best friends becomes President," I said, hoping the remark might amuse her and cheer her up a little.

She smiled but her expression was wistful as she said:

"I don't suppose anybody will ever call me Eleanor anymore."

14

Incognito

AUTHOR'S NOTE: The accounts of our long vacation motor trips, the first of which appears in this chapter, differ in some details from the stories as Mrs. Roosevelt has written them in her book *This I Remember*, published by Harper & Brothers in 1949. Since two persons rarely see things exactly the same way or remember the same things, Mrs. Roosevelt kindly gave me permission to write the story as I remember it.

BACK IN 1933, Mrs. Roosevelt had an idea that, having fulfilled her White House social duties, she could take a summer holiday motor trip, traveling as an ordinary tourist, not as the First Lady of the Land. She believed that the press and the public would respect her wishes and leave her alone.

She invited me to take a motor trip with her in July to Quebec and around the Gaspé Peninsula in Canada.

"I hear it is a lovely trip and very interesting," she said. "I'd like to see it. Wouldn't you?"

I accepted her invitation, and, although her idea that the press and public would treat her as an ordinary tourist seemed rather naïve to me, I did not tell her so. If her husband felt skeptical about it, I don't recall that he said so—not at that time.

Naturally the Secret Service didn't like it at all. They wanted to send a man along, but, since she would not let her husband ask the Secret Service for protection for her, they could not force it on her.

Gloomily they predicted that we'd be kidnaped. It was only a little more than a year since the Lindbergh baby had been kidnaped, and kidnaping was still very much on the minds of all police officials.

To Mrs. Roosevelt and to me the idea of anybody trying to kidnap two women, one nearly six feet tall and the other weighing close to two hundred pounds, seemed funny.

"Where would they hide us?" Mrs. Roosevelt demanded. "They certainly couldn't cram us into the trunk of a car!"

Only once, after his futile attempt the day after the man in Miami tried to shoot him, did the President, as I recall it, request Mrs. Roosevelt to accept Secret Service protection. Once, several years after our first trip, we planned to motor down the newly opened highway to Mexico City. We were not going alone. My friends, Mr. and Mrs. Edward S. Ely, from Massachusetts, were going with us. But this time the President put his foot down. No Secret Service, no trip, he ruled. We did not make the trip. I've always thought Ted Ely must have been relieved!

Eventually the Secret Service gave Mrs. Roosevelt a gun and a badge authorizing her to carry it. She learned to shoot, but the gun—when she remembered to take it along—was always unloaded and locked in its case, which in turn was locked in the glove compartment of the car. She was afraid some child might get hold of it.

We did not carry a gun on that first trip, but we did have a camera, a very expensive camera someone had given to Mrs. Roosevelt. Our trip took us all over northern New York and most of New England, as well as up to Quebec and around the Gaspé Peninsula. All the pictures we took of the beautiful landscapes turned out fuzzy, and in every single picture we took of each other we somehow managed to cut off the subject's head!

I had left the AP and the newspaper business when we started on our trip. Upon our return to Washington a month later I took a job with Harry Hopkins, who had become head of the newly organized Federal Emergency Relief Administration, which the newspaper headline writers called FERA.

Mrs. Roosevelt and I started out from New York on July 6. One of my most pleasant recollections is of a night we spent somewhere in the Adirondacks near the beginning of our trip. We had intended to stay that night in Lake Placid, but as it was getting dusk we passed a new little house in the woods, with a sign on the front stating that tourists would be welcomed. Mrs. Roosevelt stopped the car.

"Let's go back and try it," she suggested. "I've always wanted to stay in one of those places."

Our hosts were a very young married couple, with a

small baby. They were trying to help pay for their home by taking in tourists. After she had recovered a little from her surprise at seeing Mrs. Roosevelt walk in, our hostess told us apologetically that there would be hot water enough for only one bath. The house wasn't quite finished, and the hot-water system was not fully installed.

"Well—you're the First Lady, so you get the first bath," I said after we had been shown to our spotless little room.

In reply, Mrs. Roosevelt started thrusting her long, slender fingers in my direction. I was so ticklish that all she had to do to reduce me to a quivering mass of pulp was to point her fingers at me. She finally consented to take the first bath, however, but she must have taken it cold. For when I turned on the water for mine, it was warm.

Mrs. Roosevelt had brought along on the trip a copy of one of her favorite books, Stephen Vincent Benét's *John Brown's Body*. Evenings and during our rest periods at lunch time, she read the whole book to me. I still have that volume, somewhat battered from having traveled about for a month with our baggage in the rumble seat of her convertible.

She had already read the first part to me—about John Brown, his raid on Harpers Ferry and his execution. So the next morning we made a pilgrimage to John Brown's grave, near Lake Placid.

Late that afternoon we had a beautiful drive down a chain of islands in the center of Lake Champlain and into Burlington, Vermont. About twenty miles from

Burlington is Mount Mansfield, more than 4,000 feet high. There was then a small hotel on the top of Mount Mansfield, and tourists who dared attempt the drive up would spend the night there and watch the sunrise—a fantastic sight, with the sun shining on the mountain top while the country down below was still in darkness. This was something, too, which Mrs. Roosevelt had always wanted to do.

It was pitch dark when we arrived in a village at the foot of the mountain, but—to the horror of the town's one policeman and the rest of the inhabitants—Mrs. Roosevelt announced that she was going to drive up just the same.

It was a narrow road, with steep grades and so many hairpin turns that I lost count of them. Very few women had ever driven up that mountain, and no woman had ever attempted it in the dark. They argued and argued with Mrs. Roosevelt, to no avail. Not only did she drive up Mount Mansfield that night, but she did it in second gear. Almost any other motorist, especially after dark, would have put the car into low gear, to get all possible power out of the engine. And in low gear she could have driven more slowly. Mrs. Roosevelt those days was a superb driver.

For several days we wandered happily about in Vermont and New Hampshire. We encountered no reporters, and nobody bothered us. I thought people did not recognize her, but she explained humorously:

"My dear, they're all Republicans up here."

Somewhere in the White Mountains we had lunch with Johnny, who was teaching riding in a boys' camp.

And she took me to see the Great Stone Face, immortalized in Hawthorne's story, which I had read as a child. I was disappointed. The rock did resemble a man's head, but it was too small! I had expected it to cover the whole side of a mountain.

Our quarters in Quebec were in marked contrast to those we occupied on some other stops on that trip. We had a gorgeous suite at the Château Frontenac.

The one place I wanted to see in Quebec was the Plains of Abraham—site of the battle for Canada between Wolfe and Montcalm. So the morning after our arrival we hired a high-wheeled, horse-drawn carriage and drove out there. We saw the narrow path right up the side of a cliff, where the British had climbed in the night, dragging their artillery with them. And in my mind's eye I could see the dashing, handsomely uniformed General Montcalm galloping back and forth on his black charger in the dawn, vainly trying to rally his surprised and demoralized French and Indian troops, until he fell, mortally wounded.

In Quebec we unpacked our bags completely for the first time since we had left New York, had some pressing done and attended a formal luncheon given in Mrs. Roosevelt's honor by the Lieutenant Governor of the Province of Quebec at his home outside the city. I remember that luncheon for three things: some delicious wild strawberries we had for dessert; a wonderful, very light, delicate French wine, of which our host was justifiably proud, for it is almost impossible to ship a wine like that across the Atlantic; and his thoughtfulness in seating next to me a man who spoke English.

Everyone else—including, of course, Mrs. Roosevelt—spoke French. Unfortunately I did not.

Before we started around the Gaspé Peninsula, we stopped at the famous Shrine of Ste. Anne de Beaupré and saw the huge stack of crutches and canes left behind by the pilgrims who had gone there to ask her help.

Here we ran into a dilemma. Mrs. Roosevelt, on motor trips, used to wear a very sensible costume—a dark blue, noncrushable linen skirt and a white blouse. And around her head, over the inevitable hair net, she wore a white silk scarf, making it a kind of bandeau, with a bow in the rear. She used to wear it when she rode horseback, too. I dont' remember what I wore, but I always went bareheaded. To get into the church, we had to have some sort of covering on our heads.

For Mrs. Roosevelt, her bandeau would do. But I had no hat, no head-covering of any kind. After some thought, Mrs. Roosevelt solved the problem. She tied knots in the four corners of her handkerchief and pinned it to the top of my head with a hairpin. I must have looked funny, for I can still see her, laughing until she cried!

Most of the villages on the Peninsula looked alike—little houses clustered around a church, each house with an outdoor stone oven, in which bread was baked. The church was important to those people, not only for its spiritual value, but because it brought into their lives the only color and drama they knew. Only French was spoken in most of the villages. I had the feeling of being in a foreign country, not in North America. Mrs.

Roosevelt said it reminded her of rural France. The scenery was lovely.

In one place we met a priest who quite obviously had never heard of President Franklin D. Roosevelt, whose name for months had been on the front pages of newspapers all over the world! They never saw any newspapers up there.

When she told him her name was Roosevelt, he asked her if she was related to President Theodore Roosevelt. He was very much interested when she replied that she was Theodore Roosevelt's niece. But he asked no more questions.

So far as we knew, only twice during the entire trip around the peninsula was Mrs. Roosevelt recognized by the people who lived there as the wife of the President.

One Sunday, in one of the larger towns, we went to mass in the Roman Catholic church. (I had managed to buy a scarf for my head.) Since only French was spoken, I could not understand what the priest was saying, but at one point in the service I noticed that Mrs. Roosevelt was blushing.

"He was praying for us, by name," she explained later.

Apparently, however, his parishioners were much more interested in Mrs. Roosevelt's car than they were in Mrs. Roosevelt. For when we came out of the church, a crowd had gathered around it, examining every detail. They had never seen a convertible with the top down before.

With special fondness do I recall a lovely little inn, where we spent our last night on the Peninsula. It was run by English Canadians, and we had the whole place to ourselves.

"I don't understand it," I said to the proprietor. "Your place is so attractive, I should think it would be crowded every night during the tourist season."

He looked a little embarrassed for a moment, then explained:

"A lot of American tourists wanted to stop here tonight. They had heard that Mrs. Roosevelt was on the Peninsula, and they thought she would probably stay here tonight. But I told them we were filled up and sent them all away. I thought Mrs. Roosevelt might like to have a little privacy."

As a matter of fact, on the whole trip, so far, we had not been bothered, either by tourists or the press. Mrs. Roosevelt did see the reporters in Quebec, but they were most polite and considerate and did not try to follow us.

After the lovely scenery along the Gaspé Peninsula, our drive down through New Brunswick to Maine was depressing. The whole countryside had been ravaged by forest fires, and we drove mile after mile through stark, charred trees without any branches.

Our last night in Canada we stayed in a tourist camp —something else Mrs. Roosevelt had always wanted to do. It was a very comfortable tourist camp, with clean, attractive log cabins, each with a huge stone fireplace. The food was excellent, and, to her great satisfaction, Mrs. Roosevelt was able to buy a Maine newspaper. It was the first newspaper she had seen since we left Quebec.

We crossed the border into Maine at Presque Isle the following afternoon, and, to our horror, we found a parade lined up to meet us. Mrs. Roosevelt has often described how I looked, with some white cream smeared all over my face. We had driven all the way with the top down, and I had a rather severe sunburn. Mrs. Roosevelt's skin didn't burn—it tanned. But her lower lip burned, and it was swollen to almost twice its natural size. And we were wind-blown, dusty and dirty.

Children were lined up along the sidewalks waving flags as we drove down the main street, the procession falling in behind us. In her embarrassment and confusion, Mrs. Roosevelt bumped into a portable traffic standard that had been set up in the middle of the street. As she did so, she came out with an exasperated and quite audible "Damn!" It is a word I had never heard her use before, nor did I ever again in all the years we were friends. But, oh, how her husband enjoyed that story when we told it to him!

We finally reached the other side of the town, where we stopped; the mayor and some other officials made speeches, and Mrs. Roosevelt graciously thanked them for an enormous bouquet, which we propped up on the seat between us.

We had intended to spend that night in Houlton, Maine, but as we left Presque Isle a dozen or more cars started to follow us.

"We've got to get out of this some way," Mrs. Roosevelt said desperately. "I don't think we can stay at the hotel in Houlton. Do you?"

"They'll follow us there, I'm sure," I replied.

We drove to Houlton, but by some highly skillful maneuvering around several corners, Mrs. Roosevelt got away from the procession, and presently we were on the other side of the town, driving through the fertile potato country of Aroostook County, Maine, with the road to ourselves.

The sun was about to set when we passed a neat, prosperous-looking white farmhouse, with a sign welcoming overnight tourists.

"Shall we try it?" Mrs. Roosevelt asked.

"It looks good to me," I replied.

She turned the car around, and we drove back and into the yard. Leaving Mrs. Roosevelt in the car, I went in and asked the farmer's wife if she had room for us. She did, so I went out and got Mrs. Roosevelt, and we were shown to our rooms by our hostess. It turned out that we were the only guests in the house that night.

I came downstairs ahead of Mrs. Roosevelt, and the farmer's wife shoved a register at me. I hesitated, then said:

"If you don't mind, I think it might be better if we registered in the morning, just before we leave."

She looked surprised and wanted to know why.

"Don't you know who the lady is?" I asked her.

"Why, no," she said, shaking her head.

"It's Mrs. Roosevelt," I told her.

For a moment, I thought the woman was going to collapse. She just looked at me, without uttering a word. Quietly I opened the screen door and slipped out. Presently Mrs. Roosevelt joined me.

I told her what had happened and suggested that we

take a little walk to permit the woman to recover from the shock.

"They may throw us out when we get back," Mrs. Roosevelt remarked as we strolled down the road—for once, she walked slowly enough so that I had no trouble keeping up with her. "You can be sure of one thing. Those people did not vote for Franklin!"

We returned and sat down in a swing on the porch, awaiting developments. We had not been there long when the farmer appeared and seated himself—rather gingerly, I thought—on the steps. His curiosity had got the better of him. Then something happened that filled me with a kind of awe—something I shall never forget.

Mrs. Roosevelt had spent only a few moments going through the Maine newspaper she had bought in New Brunswick that morning. Of course it contained—as all Maine papers do—potato prices. But I almost fell out of the swing when I heard Mrs. Franklin D. Roosevelt, wife of the President of the United States, discussing potato crops and prices with that farmer as easily and confidently as though she had spent her whole life raising potatoes in Aroostook County, Maine!

Completely fascinated, I listened as she managed with deft, adroit questions to extract from him all sorts of information which, a few minutes later, she would blandly toss back to him without his realizing that she was only repeating things he himself had told her!

Maine farmers are apt to be taciturn individuals, but that Maine farmer certainly wasn't taciturn—not that evening. And I could see his respect and admiration for Mrs. Roosevelt growing, minute by minute.

When I complimented her later on her performance, Mrs. Roosevelt laughed and said:

"It was only a trick—something I learned to do when I was very young, to cover my ignorance."

But it was certainly a trick that required some extraordinarily quick thinking and a remarkable memory.

Finally the farmer's wife appeared and sat down in a rocking chair, and before long she, too, had entered into the conversation.

The evening ended around eleven o'clock, with the four of us in the kitchen, having doughnuts and milk.

15

Arthurdale

WE HAD EXPECTED TO LEAVE the Maine farm early the following morning, and our host indicated that he understood and would abide by Mrs. Roosevelt's desire for privacy. At breakfast our hostess told us traffic past the house had been unusually heavy during the night. Apparently the press and some of the tourists were still hunting for Mrs. Roosevelt. But we were sound asleep, and her car was safely hidden somewhere behind the barn, at our host's suggestion.

He was seemingly unable however to keep her visit entirely secret, for before we had finished breakfast some of his friends and neighbors drove in. Of course they wanted to meet Mrs. Roosevelt and show her their farms, too, so we were delayed in getting away. But it was a pleasant experience, and again I was amazed at the knowledge she displayed in discussing with them their hopes, their plans and their problems.

The rest of our trip was uneventful, and enjoyable. Nobody bothered us at all. We spent a couple of nights near Skowhegan, Maine, where my actress friend Jean Dixon, who later became Mrs. Ely, was appearing in summer stock. We drove up to Campobello. Tommy was spending her vacation there with some friends.

I sometimes think I may be the only person who ever visited Campobello when there was no fog. The weather while we were there was clear and cool, and the scenery had a kind of unearthly beauty.

We had to leave Campobello sooner than we wanted to because Mrs. Roosevelt had a speaking engagement at Chautauqua, away down in the southwest corner of New York State. Our vacation drew to a close as we drove down through New England and New York, stopping overnight in Portland and Albany. Upon our arrival at Chautauqua, Mrs. Roosevelt again took up her duties as First Lady of the Land.

Except for the one incident at Presque Isle, Maine, the trip had gone as she had planned it. Of course there had been some formalities and a meeting with the press in Quebec, but we had both expected that, and the Canadians were so considerate that we had enjoyed our visit. To her own satisfaction at least, Mrs. Roosevelt had demonstrated that she could travel on a vacation most of the time unnoticed, as an ordinary tourist.

Whenever Mrs. Roosevelt had been on a trip, dinner at the White House the night of her return was informal, with no outsiders, so that she could tell her husband all about what she had seen. That night for the first time I heard her give him one of those reports he had taught her to make while he was Governor of New York—reports she would make so many, many times during the years she traveled about this country and overseas as his eyes and his ears.

As he questioned her closely about what she had seen and heard, especially in Maine, I was astonished by the things she had observed that I had not noticed at all. She could, for instance, get some idea of the prosperity of a family by the wash hanging on a line in the back yard!

The dinner, however, was not taken up entirely with serious matters. Several times the President's great, booming laugh filled the dining room. For instance, when she told him how funny I looked with her handkerchief pinned to the top of my head. And when I told him about the explosive "Damn" she let out as we drove down the main street in a parade at Presque Isle.

Immediately after our return, I started out on my new job with Harry Hopkins. I had been hired to travel about the country, watching what was happening to people on relief—physically, mentally and emotionally—and trying to find out when the husbands were going to get back their jobs. I wrote long confidential reports to Mr. Hopkins, which he sent to the President, who would pass them on to members of his Cabinet and to other department heads who might be interested. I held the job for three years, and I think I probably talked with more people on relief than anyone else in the world ever did. I learned to drive, acquired an automobile and motored most of the time, alone. Very few of the relief clients I met ever knew I was from Washington.

I took the job partly because Mrs. Roosevelt wanted me to take it. She was, even in those early days of her husband's administration, probably one of the best informed and most understanding citizens in the country on the plight of the unemployed. While most of us preferred to look away from it, Mrs. Roosevelt, as the wife of the Governor of New York, had watched with great sympathy what was happening to families, had talked with hundreds of job-seekers and had contributed generously to some of them as individuals and to the charitable organizations that were trying to help them.

Harry Hopkins was an experienced and highly respected social worker, but he had an understanding of people on relief that many social workers never were able to acquire. They had been taught to deal with "problem families." But in the FERA and, later, the WPA, we were not dealing with "problem families." The great majority of the people on relief were respectable citizens, who, through no fault of their own, were obliged to have help from the government. Some of them had been very prosperous before the Great Depression set in.

One day just before I started on my first trip, Harry Hopkins said to me:

"When you are talking with a relief client, just say to yourself: 'But for the grace of God, I'd be sitting on the other side of this table.' "

I found out later that he said that to all his field representatives before they started out.

My first trip took me into Pennsylvania, and while I was in Philadelphia I stopped one day at the office of the Quaker organization, the American Friends Service Committee. There I met Clarence Pickett, its executive secretary.

"If you want to see just how bad things are," he told me, "go down to the southwestern part of the state and into West Virginia."

And he sent his brother-in-law with me.

The visit was illuminating and shocking. The Great Depression had never really hit me personally at all—not as it had those people. At the AP I had had to take a salary cut, along with everybody else, but it hadn't really hurt.

In southwestern Pennsylvania I found towns in which there was no merchandise in the stores, and nobody would have been able to buy it if there had been. The steel mills were shut down, and the coal mines operating only one or two days a week—if at all.

I remember one little town where the Roman Catholic priest told me he frequently had to gather his flock into the church for a novena.

"Sometimes it's the only way I can keep them from going crazy," he said.

And he begged me for some aspirin for his parishioners. In my report to Harry Hopkins I wrote:

"I'm still haunted by the troubled expression in his eyes."

But when I arrived in West Virginia, I decided that those people in Pennsylvania were prosperous by comparison—even the men near Uniontown, whom I had found living in abandoned coke ovens!

Scott's Run, a coal-mining community, not far from

Morgantown, was the worst place I'd ever seen. In a gutter, along the main street through the town, there was stagnant, filthy water, which the inhabitants used for drinking, cooking, washing, and everything else imaginable. One either side of the street were ramshackle houses, black with coal dust, which most Americans would not have considered fit for pigs. And in those houses every night children went to sleep hungry, on piles of bug-infested rags, spread out on the floor. There were rats in those houses.

As I proceeded through the state I found other places just as bad. Everywhere, grimy, undernourished, desperate people—so hungry that they could not wait for the vegetables to mature in the pathetic little gardens they tried to raise on mountainsides so steep that they must have had to shoot the seeds in to make them stick. They would dig up the tiny potatoes long before they had reached their full size and pick the tomatoes and eat them while they were still green.

The state relief administrator was a major in the National Guard. He had "borrowed" the National Guard camp, managed to get hold of a little money and arranged for several hundred of the most undernourished children to spend a couple of weeks there. One night, he told me, a little boy asked anxiously:

"Do we get three meals tomorrow, too?"

While I was in Logan there was an epidemic of diphtheria. One day they brought a little girl into town to have a tube inserted in her throat so she could breathe. They had to do it in a garage. In the whole state of West Virginia there was not one single free hospital bed.

I wrote about these things in reports to Harry Hopkins and in long, almost daily letters to Mrs. Roosevelt. I was in a kind of state of shock. I just couldn't believe that in this great, still potentially rich country in which I had grown up, such conditions existed.

But Mrs. Roosevelt was not surprised. She had not been down there, but she had heard about such conditions—partly through her mail, which was almost as heavy as the President's was. Sometimes she would get as many as four hundred letters in one day! Tommy was swamped and had to have help.

She had also heard about conditions in West Virginia from the Women's Trade Union League, of which she was a member. Long before her husband became President she had sent contributions to the League, which was trying to help some miners who had been black-listed following an abortive strike near Logan. Those miners and their families had been living in tents for years when I was there—and the tents were so old and tattered that they provided practically no shelter at all.

"Get those families out of those tents before Christmas," President Roosevelt told his wife when he heard about them.

And, with the help of the Quakers and Harry Hopkins, it was done.

I had been in West Virginia about a week, I think, when one night I received a telephone call from Mrs. Roosevelt from the White House. She was driving down,

she announced, and asked me to meet her in Morgantown.

I immediately sent for Clarence Pickett. I had been
very much impressed with the work of the Quakers,
who seemed to have a more practical approach to the
problem than anyone else. They couldn't do much—
their funds were limited—but they tried to help the
people to help themselves. They promoted a garden and
canning program, frequently using the most primitive
equipment. They helped the women make clothes out
of material sent down by the Red Cross, often without
thread or buttons. They helped the men make furniture
out of any wood they could find. They did little talking,
but they worked—right down among the people.

Mr. Pickett was in Morgantown when Mrs. Roosevelt arrived. I think I introduced them, and thus began
her long association with the American Friends Service
Committee, to which through the years she contributed
thousands and thousands of dollars.

Some of the listless, famished residents of Scott's Run
may have wondered a little the next day about the tall,
slender woman in a dark blue skirt and white blouse,
with a white bandeau around her head, who walked
among them, asking questions and listening attentively
to their hopeless replies. But they did not recognize her.
The Quakers, including Mr. Pickett, did not treat her
with the exaggerated formality usually accorded the
First Lady. To them, she was a friend, who had come to
help them. And they needed help—a lot of it.

I did not return to Washington with Mrs. Roosevelt,
but after hearing her story, her husband and Louis

Howe swung into action. The government purchased a 1,200-acre run-down estate near Morgantown that had belonged to a family named Arthur. The land was divided into small plots—from two to five acres. Prefabricated houses were purchased and set up, because they could be provided quickly. They were not entirely satisfactory. Prefabricated housing was then in its infancy. But those houses were infinitely better than the filthy, rat-ridden, tumble-down shacks in Scott's Run. Each family was given a cow, a pig, some chickens and seed to plant for a garden.

At first, the families were moved in free. Some years later, when they became more prosperous, they paid a little rent. And still later they were permitted to buy their homes.

At first fifty families were moved in—later the number increased to 165. The Quakers, who knew the families, selected them, preference going to those in greatest need and to those most likely to succeed. And within a few months a new community had come into being in West Virginia. It was called Arthurdale.

"You and Eleanor ought to get a great sense of satisfaction," Louis Howe said to me one day. "You really started something!"

Arthurdale was an experiment. It had its ups and its downs, as all experiments must have. The same thing happened with other, similar experiments tried out by Harry Hopkins. Once he moved several dozen relief families, who had been trying to farm on miserable cut-over timberland in northern Michigan up to a great fertile valley in Alaska. That experiment wasn't entirely successful either, but some of the families succeeded and became prosperous.

An important factor in West Virginia, which the Quakers, I believe, were the first to recognize and try to meet, was that coal mining in that area was no longer profitable. The mines were worked out. In some places the vein was only thirty inches in diameter. The miners had to work lying on their stomachs, and they would get calluses on their backs where they rubbed against the top of the vein.

Arthurdale had its bad times—and whenever it did, Mrs. Roosevelt got the blame and was criticized. It was "her baby," the critics would say. But several years later Mrs. Roosevelt went back to Arthurdale for a visit. She found that more than seventy per cent of the original families or their descendants still lived there. They had raised their families there, and their homes were paid for.

The men still worked in the mines—when they could. Coal miners are like steel workers. Coal mining is in their blood. So many times I've met coal miners and steel workers whose fathers and grandfathers before them worked in the mines or in the mills. But the husbands and fathers in Arthurdale no longer had to depend wholly on a dying industry for a living. And the younger generation had never known a place called Scott's Run.

Another thing Mrs. Roosevelt did after that trip to West Virginia. With her friend Mrs. Leonard Elmhirst, she established in Logan a free clinic and hospital for children. The two women supported it themselves,

Mrs. Roosevelt contributing money she earned from radio appearances. The hospital was small—only a few beds. But at least, no more sick children in Logan had to have operations in garages.

Mrs. Franklin D. Roosevelt was finding the job of being a President's wife somewhat different from what she had expected it to be—although it still had its drawbacks. She never overcame her dislike of living, as she used to express it, "in a goldfish bowl."

16

White House Guest

DURING PRESIDENT ROOSEVELT's first term I spent many weekends at the White House. And I usually stayed there when my job brought me in off the road for staff conferences and new assignments.

They were pleasant visits—many of them most delightful—with one exception. I still cannot think about that visit without feeling embarrassed.

Toward the end of June 1933, right after I left the AP, I had to spend a week in Washington getting indoctrinated for my new job. After that I took a month's leave of absence without pay and went on the Gaspé Peninsula trip with Mrs. Roosevelt.

While I was with the government, I always took a leave without pay when I went on a vacation trip with Mrs. Roosevelt. I did not want it said that I enjoyed any special privileges because of my friendship with her.

The President and Mrs. Roosevelt were at Campobello during that week I spent in Washington. Mrs. Roosevelt had motored up to open the house for the summer, and the President, with Jimmy, Franklin, Jr., and Johnny had sailed up the coast on the schooner *Amberjack II.*

Some other woman in her position might have sent a staff up to open the place. But such an idea would not even have occurred to Mrs. Roosevelt. It had always been her job to open the house for the summer, and it was characteristic for her to keep on doing it even though she was also mistress of the White House.

It was natural, too, for her to invite me to stay at the White House that week even though she would not be there. This she would have done for any close friend, and she frequently did. One of her friends who frequently stayed at the White House in later years while she was away, was the late Alexander Woollcott, and once, upon her return, he met her at the door with the greeting:

"Welcome, Mrs. Roosevelt. Come right in. I am delighted to see you. Make yourself at home."

Since the weather was very hot, Mrs. Roosevelt had instructed Ike Hoover to put me in her sitting room, which was supposedly air-conditioned. Portable air-conditioners were then in the experimental stage. The machine in Mrs. Roosevelt's sitting room was a large, rectangular steel tank, set in the fireplace. Underneath it was a pan, which had to be emptied periodically, like the pan under the old-fashioned icebox.

The first night I was there one of the men servants came in about eleven o'clock and emptied the pan.

Whereupon I opened both windows—I couldn't understand why they were closed—and went to bed.

When I awoke in the morning, the water on the floor in Mrs. Roosevelt's sitting room looked at least three inches deep! My bedroom slippers were floating on it, like little boats. It was seeping under the closed doors into the President's bedroom, into the little hall between her sitting room and bedroom and out into the West Hall.

In Mrs. Roosevelt's sitting room there was a large and very beautiful light blue rug. While I was toying with my breakfast out in the West Hall—I had no appetite that morning—I saw them carry out the rug, a dripping, sodden mess, while a crew of men were at work inside with mops.

"I'm moving to a hotel," I announced when Ike Hoover appeared. He looked shocked.

"You can't do that to me," he said.

"What do you mean?" I asked. "Why should my moving to a hotel affect you?"

"Because," he replied earnestly, "if you did, Miss Eleanor would never forgive me."

Ike would sometimes forget and refer to Mrs. Roosevelt by the name he had called her when her Uncle Ted was President. It was a term of affection, not in any way disrespectful.

"She told me," he added, "that you were to stay here, and that I was to do everything possible to make you comfortable. If you move out, she will think I didn't carry out her orders."

Reluctantly I agreed to stay on, but only if that

machine was turned off—and not turned on again while I was there.

Ike then explained to me that the machine was actually a dehumidifier. With the windows open, I had been trying to dehumidify the whole city of Washington.

Since Mrs. Roosevelt's sitting room was right over the state dining room, I was worried about the ceiling down there.

"Has the water gone down there?" I asked Ike.

He shook his head, but I didn't quite believe him. And for a couple of days, every time I went in or out of the White House, I'd sneak into the state dining room and take a look at the ceiling. But there were no damp spots. Eventually they managed to get Mrs. Roosevelt's rug dried out, but there was always a slight ripple in it as long as it was there—and I think it was still on the floor when she moved out.

I hate to think how many sheets of White House writing paper I wasted that evening, struggling with my confession to Mrs. Roosevelt. But I finally got it written and mailed. To my great relief, she seemed more amused than annoyed by my misadventure.

Mrs. Roosevelt arrived back in Washington a couple of days ahead of the President, who had come down the coast from Maine on the U.S. cruiser *Indianapolis*. The ship anchored off the Maryland coast the night of July 3, and the following day we motored down to Annapolis and celebrated the Fourth by lunching with him aboard the cruiser. Louis Howe was in the party—he had a special interest in the *Indianapolis*, for she was named after

the city where he was born. The rest of the group included Missy, Tommy, some other house guests and me.

At lunch I discovered, to my consternation, that Mrs.
Roosevelt had told the President about my encounter
with the dehumidifier. But he, too, seemed to think
it was funny, and thereafter he always referred to the
contraption as "Hick's rugwashing machine." Before
long it was removed.

For a few days, the President teased me about it—always when there were other guests present. The other
guests would include some important people, by whom
I was greatly awed.

At some point during lunch or dinner, the President
would raise his head, sniff and remark:

"It seems to me that Washington is a little less
humid than it was."

Then, with a significant look at me:

"What do *you* think, Hick?"

"I think you are right, Mr. President," I would answer meekly.

He never pursued the subject further, but I was by
no means sure he wouldn't.

After lunch on the *Indianapolis* that Fourth of July
we all drove back to the White House and dined that
evening on the South veranda, where we watched the
fireworks display, set off at the base of the Washington
Monument. About fireworks the President was like a
small boy.

"It didn't last long enough," he complained after it
was over.

I recall some rather unique experiences during my

White House visits. Once—I never knew how it happened—I actually had dinner alone with the President and Mrs. Roosevelt. Just the three of us, in front of the fireplace in her sitting room. With a large family of their own and many relatives and friends, the President and Mrs. Roosevelt rarely dined alone, or with a single guest. They were exceedingly hospitable and liked to have company.

That night the President told me:

"Never get into an argument with the Missis. You can't win. You think you have her pinned down here (thumping the table with his forefinger) but she bobs right up away over there somewhere! No use—you can't win."

I recall some weekend trips on the old *Sequoia*, which belonged to the Department of the Interior, but which was used as the presidential yacht until the *Potomac* was acquired. One trip in particular, when the only passengers were the President, his naval aide, Mrs. Roosevelt and I.

Two other ships followed the *Sequoia* as we cruised down Chesapeake Bay. One was for the Secret Service men, the other for the newspaper correspondents.

The Secret Service men had brought along a speedboat, and on a warm, sunny Saturday afternoon the President took his wife, his naval aide, Captain Vernou, and me for a ride in it. He handled it expertly, of course—and at times we went very fast. Whenever we were near the shore, I worried a little about "deadheads"—logs or trees floating just beneath the surface. But I finally said to myself:

"Well, if you get drowned, kid, you'll be in good company."

Anyway, I thought the President, who was a wonderful swimmer, would probably keep me afloat if we did capsize. Those days he could beat any of his boys across the White House swimming pool. Once in a game of water polo in the pool at Hyde Park, he knocked one of the newspaper correspondents out cold, dragged him out and revived him! With apologies.

It may have been on that trip, while we were sitting out on deck, reading the Sunday papers, I got up and started to move away.

"Where are you going?" Mrs. Roosevelt asked.

"Downstairs," I replied innocently.

"Below, Hick! Below!" the President bellowed. "I'll make a sailor out of you if I have to . . ."

He did not complete the sentence, leaving me to imagine the horrible consequences.

Another weekend I remember was cold and rainy. The weather—I think it was in the fall—had been bad for several days. After we had said good-by to the luncheon guests and had returned to her sitting room that Sunday afternoon, Mrs. Roosevelt said:

"I've got to get Franklin out of this house. He hasn't been out for a week."

She looked thoughtful and added:

"I wonder if he'd like to go out to Normandy Farms for tea."

Normandy Farms was a delightful country restaurant in Maryland, about fifteen miles from Washington. Mrs.

Roosevelt liked to go out there for lunch or tea, taking Mrs. Henry Morgenthau, Jr., Tommy or me along.

"I think I'll ask him," she said and went into his study.

The President, it developed, would like very much indeed to go out to Normandy Farms for tea—but with one stipulation.

"I'd love it," he said, "but only if I can ride out there with you, in your car, just the two of us, with you driving."

Whereupon the Secret Service proceeded to go into what Mrs. Roosevelt called a "tizzie." But the President "had his Dutch up," as she would say.

"The Secret Service may follow us in another car," he said, "but they've got to stay at least half a block behind us. And they've all got to be inside—nobody on the running boards."

Colonel Starling, head of the White House Secret Service detail, hurried over from the Mayflower, where he lived.

"How about letting Gus Gennerich ride in the rumble seat?" he suggested. The President had brought Gus, who had been his bodyguard in Albany, down from New York, and Gus was always nearby, even in the White House.

"No," the President replied. "Either I go with my Missis alone, in her car, or I don't go. That's all."

What he was proposing was actually against the law. After the assassination of William McKinley, Congress passed a law, making it obligatory for a President to have Secret Service protection, whether he liked it or not. Some of them didn't like it—particularly Calvin Coolidge, who delighted in slipping away from the Secret Service men.

Finally the Secret Service reluctantly gave in, and we started off. First the President and Mrs. Roosevelt in her little blue convertible, then, half a block behind, a big black car filled with Secret Service men and in the rear a White House limousine with Missy LeHand and me. There were no other house guests.

The weather was so bad that the streets were deserted. I don't think Mrs. Roosevelt drove over twenty-five miles an hour all the way, and she stopped at every red light and scrupulously obeyed all traffic rules.

Normandy Farms had no other guests that afternoon, although it was usually crowded on a Sunday. The President was not wearing his leg braces, and, as two of the Secret Service men carried him in, Missy and I stood on either side of the entrance whistling "Hail to the Chief," the march the bands always play when a President appears. It was Missy's idea, not mine! He made faces at us as he passed, and presently he got even with me.

Naturally, the staff at Normandy Farms was thrown into confusion when the President of the United States appeared on a stormy Sunday afternoon for tea. Such a thing had never happened before. But they managed to get us seated, in front of a big, roaring open fire, and tea was brought in.

Then came a very much flustered young waitress with a tray of sandwiches, cookies, little cakes and pastry. In her confusion, she started to serve me first.

I frowned and shook my head in dismay. One of the hostesses came hurrying over, took the girl aside and apparently explained to her that the President is always served first, then the First Lady and finally their guests. Presently she got around to me again.

"Miss Hickok has said she doesn't care for any," the President said calmly!

Mrs. Roosevelt beckoned to the waitress and whispered to her that the President was only teasing me.

Sometimes dinner at the White House used to be an ordeal for me, for Mrs. Roosevelt and I would be doing something together, and she never allowed me enough time to get dressed. I'd end up panting and perspiring, rushing out to the elevator where the President was waiting—you are never supposed to keep the President waiting—with Mrs. Roosevelt hooking me up. I can see him now, grinning at me commiseratingly.

I recall one Sunday night supper at the White House very vividly. A couple of weeks earlier, Mrs. Roosevelt and I had spent a weekend in New York, shopping and going to the theater. I arrived in Pennsylvania station a few minutes ahead of her. She was coming in on a train from Atlantic City, where she had made a speech. I decided to wait for her.

When I went down to the platform where her train would pull in, I noticed a group of reporters. I thought they must be there to meet someone else. They had grown accustomed to her frequent trips to New York and rarely covered her. But as she stepped off the train, they crowded around her. Her head held high, she stalked through them, refusing to say a word.

"What have you done?" I asked as we drove away in a taxi.

"Oh, I sounded off on the Hauptmann case," she replied guiltily. "Franklin will be furious. It's in all the papers."

Bruno Hauptmann had been convicted and sentenced to death for the kidnaping and murder of the Lindbergh baby. The date for his execution had been set. When a reporter in Atlantic City asked Mrs. Roosevelt what she thought about it, he got an honest answer.

Mrs. Roosevelt has never believed in capital punishment, and she said she thought it was wrong to take a man's life in any case and especially after he had been convicted on circumstantial evidence only. Hauptmann had been convicted on circumstantial evidence, but the evidence against him was so convincing that I doubt if any jury would have acquitted him.

The story certainly was in all the papers—on page one. The reporter had misinterpreted her remark slightly, leaving the impression that she had referred only to Hauptmann. His lawyers took it up, and it was expected they would use her remark as part of their basis for an appeal.

Whenever the telephone rang that weekend, Mrs. Roosevelt and I would exchange apprehensive glances, expecting that her husband would call and express himself definitely and forcefully. He did call a couple of times, but he was very affable both times and did not mention the Hauptmann case.

He never did mention it until that Sunday night at supper a couple of weeks later. Mrs. Roosevelt had to leave, after she had scrambled the eggs in a chafing dish at the table, and go to a radio station to make a speech. There were no outside guests that night—only "the people in the house," as Mrs. Roosevelt used to say. "The people in the house" included Louis Howe and Missy, who both lived there, any of the children who happened to be there and a few intimate friends who were frequent guests, as I was.

With an infinitely mischievous expression on his face, the President looked at me after Mrs. Roosevelt had left and asked:

"What's the Missis going to talk about tonight, Hick? The Hauptmann case?"

Trying not to choke on the food I was swallowing, I managed to reply:

"I'm sorry, Mr. President. She didn't tell me."

"I've been good, Hick," he said with elaborate innocence. "Awfully good. I haven't said a single word about it."

And he never mentioned it again, either to Mrs. Roosevelt or to me!

As the years went by, and she gained a great deal of experience in talking to the press, Mrs. Roosevelt learned to be a little more restrained in her replies. Yet she was never evasive, as many persons in public life are. If she gave an answer, it was an honest answer. If it was a question she thought she should not answer, she said so. That is one reason why her relations with the newspaper people remained so friendly through the years. Later, she might have said that she did not feel qualified to discuss the Hauptmann case, or she might

have impressed on the reporter that she was referring
to capital punishment in general—not simply to the
Hauptmann case.

Only once do I remember having seen the President
really annoyed with his wife. That night Associate Justice Cardozo of the Supreme Court was a dinner guest.
Mrs. Roosevelt—who had given her personal maid an
evening off—got into zipper trouble, and I had to help
her. Her German shepherd, Major, who had been
trained for police work, nipped me on the elbow, because I got too close to his mistress.

When we finally got the zipper working, she sent me
out ahead of her and appeared herself a few moments
later. The President said sternly:

"Justice Cardozo is one of the most distinguished men
in this country. It's a terrible thing to keep a man like
him waiting."

The President himself had had to wait many times—
because I was late—but he had never shown any annoy-
ance at all!

Sometimes Harry Hopkins—who, of course, had a
few other things on his mind—would be very slow about
deciding where he wanted me to go next. Hanging
around Washington, even at the White House, I'd get
bored, worried and depressed. One night I remarked
bitterly to Mrs. Roosevelt:

"I'm really on relief, myself."

She smiled slightly as she observed:

"You might say it's rather luxurious relief."

I felt very much ashamed of myself and apologized.
President Roosevelt used to complain, humorously,

because the women guests seated next to him wouldn't talk to him. But I recall one woman guest who did. She was my little aunt from Illinois. She had come East with her daughter to visit my sister in New York and me, and Mrs. Roosevelt invited the four of us to the White House for a weekend.

Before dinner, the first night we were there, Mrs. Roosevelt went in to the President and said:

"Now, Franklin, you behave yourself tonight. Hick's Republican relatives are here from Illinois. Don't you say anything to shock them."

My little aunt, who was in her seventies, was soft-spoken and shy. Like most Americans, myself included, she held the President in great awe—even a Democratic President. I knew she had dreaded sitting next to him at dinner.

To my great surprise, however, she appeared to be perfectly at ease and having a grand time. I was too far away to hear what they were saying, but they were both laughing a lot. Never in all the years I knew him did I see Franklin Roosevelt put forth more charm than he did that evening.

My relatives from Illinois were Republicans all right. I doubt if my aunt ever voted for President Roosevelt.

But from that night on, let anyone utter an unkind word about Franklin D. Roosevelt, the man, and my gentle, soft-spoken little aunt would put up an argument that was truly astonishing!

17

Yosemite Safari

DURING THE WINTER following our trip around the Gaspé Peninsula, Mrs. Roosevelt began to plan our next vacation.

The President expected to go to Hawaii in July, and Mrs. Roosevelt suggested that she and I take a motor trip through some of the national parks in the Rockies and meet him in Portland, Oregon, on his return. Basing her belief on her success on our first trip, she was still confident that she could travel about unnoticed most of the time.

We met in California early in July, 1934. Stopping in Chicago to visit the World's Fair, which was in its second year, she flew to Sacramento. When she took off from Chicago, her destination was supposed to be a secret.

But when I arrived in Sacramento to spend the night and meet her plane early the following morning, I found reporters and photographers waiting in the hotel lobby. Somebody—I suspected the airline press agent—had broken her secret.

I then proceeded to do the silliest thing I ever did in my life. As the reporters undoubtedly put it, I tried to "out-smart" them.

I was really desperate, though. Our first destination was to be Colfax, a very small town north of Sacramento, where we were to spend a week with my dearest friend, Ella Morse Dickinson, and her husband. The Dickinsons couldn't put us up. Their house was too small. But Ella and I had a friend who owned a sanitarium in the hills, just outside the town, and she turned her house over to Mrs. Roosevelt and me for a week. The house was not on the sanitarium grounds, but it was close enough so that the commotion caused by the reporters and photographers and by the crowds that would inevitably be attracted by their presence would disturb the patients. We simply could not have them there.

I appealed to the hotel management for help. And they thought they could solve my problem. First they called the state police. I left my keys with the clerk, and during the night a state trooper drove my small gray convertible away and hid it. A Secret Service man accompanied him and removed my D. C. license plates, substituting California plates. He also had some Nevada and Oregon license plates, which he hid, along with mine, under the seat. Every time we crossed a state line on that trip, a Secret Service man would appear and change our license plates. Mrs. Roosevelt and I used to amuse ourselves by conjecturing about what would happen to us if we were picked up for some traffic violation, and the police found four sets of license plates and a gun in our car! She had brought her gun along, not for protection, but to shoot at targets away up in the mountains.

Early the next morning I took a cab out to the airport, followed by the reporters and photographers. Pulling on them that old familiar line, "I used to be a newspaperman myself," I asked them if they would please give Mrs. Roosevelt a chance to wash her face and have a cup of coffee before they interviewed her. They agreed. Looking as innocent as I could, I told them our first stop would be selected by Mrs. Roosevelt —I didn't know where.

We left them in the lobby, took an elevator up, then another elevator down to the rear entrance to the hotel, where we found my car, with a state trooper at the wheel. We threw our bags into the rumble seat, jumped in and started off, the state trooper driving.

We weren't even out of Sacramento when the trooper, glancing into the rear-vision mirror, announced:

"Sorry, ladies, but they're right behind us, a whole carload of 'em."

I, who had been a newspaper reporter for twenty years, had been naïve enough to believe that those reporters would not suspect a trick and cover every exit from that hotel!

As soon as we were out of the city, the state trooper put a heavy foot down on the accelerator, and with dismay I watched the speedometer go up and up and up— 50, 55, 60, 75, 77 miles an hour. Another state trooper had swung in ahead of us, flashing his red lights on and off. My car was too light to be driven at such high speed, even by a state trooper. And we were crowded, three on the seat. Also, I couldn't help wondering what was happening to my motor. The car was brand new—it had only about 100 miles on the speedometer. In the 1930s we used to break in those inexpensive cars gradually— 25 miles an hour the first 500 miles.

Mrs. Roosevelt must have been thinking along the same lines, for presently she said:

"It's no use. Let's stop."

The press drew up behind us as we pulled off the road, and the trooper who had been driving ahead came back and joined us.

"You've been most kind, and we are very grateful," Mrs. Roosevelt told the state troopers, "but I think you'd better leave us now. We'll have to find some other way out of this situation."

Of course the first question the reporters asked— while the photographers took pictures of my car—was:

"Where are you going, Mrs. Roosevelt?"

"I'm sorry, but I'm not going to tell you," she said firmly. "This is my vacation, and I expect to be treated as any other tourist would be treated. I'll answer any other questions you want to ask, if I can. But not that one."

Our destination, however, was the only subject that interested them. Mrs. Roosevelt reached around behind the seat and pulled out her knitting bag.

"It's nice here in the shade," she observed pleasantly, "and I like to knit. I'm willing to sit here all day, if I have to, but I am not going to tell you where we're go-ing."

We finally agreed to accompany them to a nearby roadside restaurant for breakfast, after which they drove away, promising not to try to follow us any more. But the photographers had pictures of my car, with the California license numbers.

Our stay in Colfax was peaceful and enjoyable. We lunched and dined with the Dickinsons, had picnics up in the mountains and some wonderful evenings, with Mrs. Roosevelt reading aloud to us from Ella's well-thumbed *Oxford Book of English Verse*. I've never known anyone else who could read poetry as beautifully as Mrs. Roosevelt did.

As we were unpacking in Colfax, Mrs. Roosevelt handed me several typewritten sheets of National Parks Service stationery. She had written me that we might take a little camping trip in the mountains, and here it was, all planned out, much more elaborate, I was sure, than anything she had had in mind. She had only asked for information and suggestions. I was a little amused until I came to this sentence:

"Miss Hickok will require a quiet, gentle horse, since she has not ridden for some time."

Miss Hickok certainly had *not* ridden for some time —not since she was a child in South Dakota and would occasionally have a chance to ride a cow pony!

"How could you do this to me?" I asked her reproach-fully.

"Oh, you'll manage," she said comfortably. "But we'll

have to stop somewhere and buy you some trousers and a shirt."

We drove from Colfax up through Donner Pass in the High Sierras and down into Nevada, where a Secret Service man attached the Nevada license plates to my car. We stopped at a country general store, where I bought some Levis and a shirt, and proceeded to the ranch of Anna's friends, Mr. and Mrs. William S. Dana.

The Dana ranch was at Pyramid Lake, surrounded by desert country, and to get there we had to drive over forty miles of the worst road I had ever seen. My little car hopped around over the bumps and in and out of the ruts like an ant on a hot griddle. But I consoled myself with the thought that we'd certainly be safe from intrusion there. And we were.

The Dana ranch was a little oasis in the desert, the house surrounded by a smooth green lawn. They had their own electric plant, which made the green lawn possible, for it could be watered by means of an electric pump. The house was charming and very comfortable.

The Danas had one servant, a man, who did the cooking, ranch style. We all pitched in and did the rest of the housework. Probably because she thought it was the most distasteful job, Mrs. Roosevelt insisted on washing the dishes. I dried them for her. She was not a very good dish-washer—she would never put enough soap in the water, and the dishes came out greasy.

For recreation, we had swimming, in Pyramid Lake, and riding. The Danas had working for them Bar Francis, an old cowboy, about seventy, who told us he had lived in a saddle since he was seven years old. Those days great herds of wild horses roamed the plains, and, when a rancher wanted a colt, he would go out and rope one and break it to bridle and saddle. Unlike many cowboys, Bar Francis would break a colt without ever laying a whip on it. As a result, the Dana horses trusted people and really liked them. When Bar Francis went out into the corral, they would come running toward him like pet dogs and would nuzzle in his pockets for treats.

He had one horse—which he had broken for our hostess, Ella Dana—of which he was particularly proud, the most beautiful palomino I ever saw. Its coat was like burnished gold, and it had a platinum-blond mane and tail. The horse's name was Pal, and Mrs. Roosevelt rode Pal every day. The first time she mounted him, Bar Francis came forward with a box for her to step up on, but she waved him away and mounted from the ground.

"You are mighty spry for a lady of your age," Bar Francis told her admiringly. Mrs. Roosevelt was still several months away from being fifty!

I had no ambition to ride, but she insisted on my trying it. Otherwise, she said, I'd get very lame when we started riding the mountain trails. A big gray horse, called Old Blue, was assigned to me. The Danas never destroyed their horses when they grew old, but simply retired them. Old Blue had been in retirement for some time. I did not mount him from the ground!

"You have to kick him to make him keep going," Bill Dana instructed me as we started out. But I certainly wasn't going to try to get any speed out of Old Blue or any other horse. After we'd ridden a short distance, however, I noticed that Old Blue stumbled a lot, apparently stepping into holes.

"Hey, Bill!" I shouted—he and Mrs. Roosevelt were some distance ahead of me—"this darned horse keeps stumbling. I'm afraid he's going to fall down!"

Bill rode back, took a look at Old Blue and threw back his head, howling with laughter.

"Hick," he gasped, "your damned horse is asleep! Kick him! Kick him hard! You have to, to keep him awake!"

I finally managed to work up enough courage to nudge Old Blue gently with my toes—just enough to keep him awake. Mrs. Roosevelt and Bill always left us far behind.

I did, however, have some rides on Old Blue that I thoroughly enjoyed—just before sunset, with Bar Francis. We always walked the horses, the reins hanging loose, while he taught me to roll cigarettes, how to tamp them out on the saddle horn, so they wouldn't set fire to the sage brush, and told me stories about his past. In his youth, he said, he had been a professional bad man, a gambler and a gun-toter. But he had later reformed and finally became a sheriff!

Two Forest Rangers from the Yosemite National Park picked Mrs. Roosevelt and me up at the Dana ranch. We rode with one of them, in the Ranger's car, while the other one drove my car. We were going into the park, they said, over some back roads through the mountains, and we'd be safer riding with someone who was used to them. For once, Mrs. Roosevelt consented, and she must have been glad she had. Some of the roads were so narrow that two cars never could have passed on them. On one side there would be a sheer cliff, rising up hundreds of feet, and the other side a drop-off that seemed to end in eternity! Frequently we were above the clouds.

Our drive ended in a valley in the park, and there we found our escorts and our equipment for the camping trip. I have a picture they took as we rode away, looking as though we were starting out on a safari somewhere in Africa. We had with us five Forest Rangers, led by the Chief Forest Ranger himself, seven saddle horses, and five pack animals, with a little burro bringing up the rear!

I had never ridden mountain trails before, nor had Mrs. Roosevelt. Some of the trails seemed to go right straight up into the air and straight down again. Going up was easier than going down—and certainly less frightening. Sometimes the trail down was so steep that I had a feeling that we were about to go off into thin air.

Mrs. Roosevelt was riding some distance ahead of me, escorted by a couple of Rangers, and I caught only occasional glimpses of her. She seemed to be perfectly relaxed and enjoying herself. She was, of course, an experienced horsewoman, having ridden since childhood. I was also reassured somewhat by the realization that the Rangers would certainly not risk the life of the President's wife by taking her over a trail that was really dangerous.

I was mounted on a little brown mare, and before long, I became so fascinated by her behavior that I forgot my fears. When we came to a very steep down trail, she would stop and survey the situation. Sometimes, if there was room, she would zigzag, going from side to side. Sometimes there wasn't room for that. Then she would reach down with one of her front hoofs and actually paw the dust off the rocks. Apparently rocks with dust on them were slippery, and she knew it.

I became very fond of the little mare and rode her all the time while we were up in the mountains. I really had to, for I was bothered by the altitude, and walking was difficult. Mrs. Roosevelt said I had altitude trouble because I smoked too much. I hated to admit it, but she was probably right.

I don't remember how high up we were when we made camp, but we were above the timber line. We camped beside a beautiful little lake that had no name, and on a mountainside right across the lake, extending almost down to the water, was a big bank of snow. The lake was lovely, but it was also very cold. Every morning Mrs. Roosevelt would dash down there and take a brief swim. I tried it once—and thought I'd never catch my breath again. It didn't bother her, though. Every morning those days she would take an ice cold shower or tub, as she had done since she was a child.

Climbing mountains, even at that altitude, didn't bother her either. One morning she and the Chief Forest Ranger climbed up to an elevation of some 13,000 feet. When they came down, I thought that Ranger was going to have a stroke. His face was purple. But Mrs. Roosevelt? You'd have thought she had come in from a stroll in Central Park in New York!

The days we spent up there were really lovely. One

of the Rangers was considered the best flapjack maker in the Yosemite. He cooked all the meals over a bonfire. Early every morning one of the men would go out casting in the lake for trout, which we had for breakfast. They were good, but I preferred the flapjacks.

The nights were enchanting. They had set up a tent for us, but we used it only as a dressing room and slept right on the ground, in sleeping bags. It's a wonderful experience to lie, warm and snug in a sleeping bag, high up in the mountains, and look at the stars.

After several days in camp, we rode back down the trails to what they called "the floor of the valley." Crossing the valley, we had to ford a little river. We were crossing on a sand bar, in very shallow water, but there was a steep drop-off on our left. Following instructions, I was not trying to guide the mare. The reins were hanging loose.

Suddenly she made a determined move to the left. I managed somehow to slide off and landed sitting down on the sand bar in water up to my chin, while my little friend went into the deep water and rolled! They had forgotten to tell me that she had one bad habit—whenever she saw some nice, cool, deep water she took a bath!

The Rangers apologetically fished us out, I mounted again, and, both dripping, we completed the ride.

Mrs. Roosevelt said later that she was frightened, but she gave no sign of it at the time. She only seemed worried lest I catch cold. I wasn't frightened at all—only embarrassed.

18

Last Attempt

ONE INCIDENT during our stay in the Yosemite National Park, after our camping trip, stands out in my memory above all others.

We stayed in a beautiful hotel, operated by the National Parks Service. The first night, while we were at dinner, who should walk into the dining room but Secretary of the Interior Harold L. Ickes.

Secretary Ickes was the last man in the world I wanted to meet at that time. He and Harry Hopkins were then engaged in a more-or-less public struggle for supremacy in providing work for the unemployed. Their programs were diametrically opposed, and each had been allocated funds by Congress to carry them out.

Under Harry Hopkins' program, with which I was associated, scores of men, horses, mules, plows, carts, picks and shovels would be put to work to build a road. Secretary Ickes used what we in the FERA derisively called "the trickle-down method." Under his program a road would be built with heavy machinery, using few men. His theory was that the use of big bulldozers and other machines would help heavy industry and provide jobs that way. It probably did—but it wasn't even felt in the area where the road was being built.

In my reports to Mr. Hopkins I had been very critical of Mr. Ickes' program, using statistics to show how few people it was putting to work, compared with our record. It took us longer to build a road, but, so far as I could see, it was just as good a road as Mr. Ickes' road. My reports went to the President—who maintained a neutral position—and I suspected he sent them to the Secretary of the Interior.

Secretary Ickes came over and joined us at dinner and was very agreeable, although he had the reputation of being extremely blunt and peppery. The two programs were not mentioned.

We were sitting out on the terrace after dinner when Mrs. Roosevelt was called away, and I found myself alone with the Secretary. I wanted to run after her, begging, "Please don't leave me alone with that man!" But of course I couldn't.

Secretary Ickes and I sat for a moment in silence. As I recall it, he was smoking a cigar. Finally he spoke.

"I've been reading your reports," he said abruptly. "Interestin'."

"Thank you, Mr. Secretary," I said weakly.

At that point Mrs. Roosevelt returned, and the subject was dropped. But I'd had some bad moments, which I have never forgotten.

I do not recall meeting any reporters in Yosemite National Park—they may have been barred. But we couldn't get away from the tourists. They followed us everywhere, in droves. And there were times when I behaved badly and embarrassed Mrs. Roosevelt.

One day we came to a place where there were chipmunks so tame they'd eat out of your hand. They were charming little creatures, and it was a delightful experience to have one of them perch on your wrist, daintily picking crumbs out of your hand. But we had just started to feed them when I realized that we were completely surrounded by tourists, all pointing cameras at us. Bending over to feed a chipmunk is not a very dignified position in which to have your picture taken, and I lost my temper. We left hastily, with Mrs. Roosevelt, as I said, trying to "shush" me.

Another bad time, for me, was the day we went to see the giant redwood trees. I've never seen anything more impressive, including even Mount Rainier and the Grand Canyon. But I felt almost prayerful, and, above all, I wanted to be quiet. However, we were surrounded, not only by tourists, but guides, who kept hurling statistics at us. What difference did it make, how tall they were or how big their trunks were? Anybody could read that in the guide book.

The final indignity, so far as I was concerned, was to name one of those trees—which was probably a sapling when Christ walked this earth—after General Sherman. Or anyone else. To me, it seemed positively sacrilegious. And I said so, right out loud. Of course I shouldn't have done that.

When we finally left the park, we had told nobody where we were going. We headed for San Francisco. This, to me, was to be the high point of the trip. I had been there several times, once spent a winter there, and loved the city. And I wanted to show Mrs. Roosevelt all my favorite spots.

I had made reservations for us in a small, inconspicuous hotel back of the St. Francis, without telling the management who my companion was to be. The desk clerk and the manager looked a little abashed when we walked in late in the afternoon, but they had recovered somewhat by the time we had unloaded the car. A man came and got the car and parked it in a nearby garage.

We were interrupted only once as we unpacked, bathed and dressed. The manager sent up some flowers. There were several letters for Mrs. Roosevelt, all addressed to me, including one or two from her husband, in Honolulu. We felt rested and relaxed as we went out to dinner.

We dined in my favorite restaurant, a small, French café, which had the quaint name "Pierre's New Frank's." I had eaten there many times, and, as the name indicated, it had once belonged to a man named Frank, who had sold it to Pierre. There was nothing noteworthy about its furnishings, or its appearance, but it served the best French food I'd ever eaten anywhere. It was patronized almost exclusively by San Franciscans. Few tourists ever found it.

In the restaurant, nobody apparently noticed us at all. The service was good—it always was—but we got no special attention.

It was Saturday night, and the streets were crowded as we walked over to take a cable car up to the top of Russian Hill. Occasionally I'd notice someone looking with a puzzled expression at the tall woman who walked beside me. But nobody paid any attention to us on the cable car.

On Russian Hill we walked up and stood for a few moments outside the apartment house where I had spent a winter with Ella Dickinson before she was married. And I pointed out the floor where we had lived, with its picture window that gave us a great sweeping view of the bay from our living room.

Then we went over to a tiny park and sat in the moonlight, quietly talking and looking at the bay, with Alcatraz Island, like a big, lighted battleship floating in the center.

Around eleven o'clock we took the cable car back down the hill, stopped at a drugstore near the St. Francis for ice cream sodas and started to walk back to our hotel. It had been a perfect evening, we agreed.

"Tomorrow night, if it isn't foggy," I told Mrs. Roosevelt, "we'll get the car and drive up to the top of Twin Peaks. The view of San Francisco at night from there is almost incredibly beautiful."

We were half a block from the hotel when the manager met us in a state of panic. Somehow word of our presence had slipped out, and his lobby was filled with reporters.

"I didn't tell anyone," he protested. "I didn't think you'd want to be bothered—if you had, you wouldn't have come to my hotel. You do believe me, don't you?"

I believed him. I had stayed at his hotel a number of times, and he and I were good friends. I did suspect the hotel's one bellboy. Feeling more charitable toward him now than I did then, I hope, if he did it, the press tipped him well. And that, if the manager found out he'd done it, he didn't fire him. It must have been too much of a temptation for the bellboy.

Through a barrage of exploding flashlights we walked through the lobby to the elevator. Mrs. Roosevelt shook her head as the reporters fired questions at her.

"I'm here on a vacation," she said. "I'd like to be left alone, if you don't mind."

The next morning we walked over to the Hotel Clift to have breakfast—our hotel had no restaurant. As we ate our cereal, a photographer crouched in front of our table, shooting flashlights right in our faces. In 1934 news photographers didn't use flashlight bulbs, but black powder, which they ignited in a metal tray. It would explode with a deafening bang and a lot of smoke.

All that day we were followed wherever we went by reporters and camera men and the crowds they attracted, to Fisherman's Wharf, on a ferry ride across the bay to Sausalito, up to the Fairmount Hotel, where we dined. We were able to exchange hardly a dozen words in private.

The following morning we went to have shampoos. The proprietor of the beauty parlor told me, when I went back there a few weeks later, that one of the customers had tried to bribe her to snip off a lock of Mrs. Roosevelt's hair, for a souvenir! Monday night, after we were finally back behind locked doors in our hotel, Mrs. Roosevelt said quietly:

"I think we may as well leave tomorrow morning. Don't you? There's a road open most of the way up the coast, I've heard. Let's take that. It doesn't go through any large towns, and the scenery must be beautiful."

I received my next shock when they brought my car around in the morning. Souvenir-hunters had found it, in the garage, and had taken everything removable—maps, sun glasses, sun-tan lotion, chocolate bars, my cigarette lighter, even a little St. Christopher medal which Mrs. Roosevelt had given me, and which I kept in the glove compartment. I was surprised to find that they hadn't taken the hub caps, too.

I realize now that it was a mistake for Mrs. Roosevelt, wife of the President of the United States, to try to visit San Francisco as an ordinary tourist. Years later I found out that some people in San Francisco had never forgiven her for "sneaking in," as they said, and staying at "that dreadful, cheap hotel." The hotel was not so expensive as the St. Francis, the Fairmount or the Palace (the Mark Hopkins hadn't been built when we were there), but it was clean and comfortable and respectable. Its only fault was that it was inconspicuous. But they found us anyway—after one lovely evening.

The trip up the coast was leisurely and beautiful. Since we had left San Francisco earlier than we had planned, we took a side trip and spent a night in Crater Lake National Park, a really fascinating place. In the center of the lake is the top of a long-extinct, sunken volcano, and the water around it is a deep, deep blue.

We also visited Muir Woods and saw some more big trees, not so old or with such huge trunks as those we had seen before, but taller. And this time we were alone. We hardly spoke to each other as we walked about among them. Trees so beautiful and so majestic—so tall that we'd have had to lie down flat on our backs to see the tops—make a person feel reverent.

Our last night before we arrived in Portland we spent in a small city in Oregon, called Bend. We found a very good hotel there and were given a suite. Since we were staying only overnight and would have to leave early the following morning, we did little unpacking, although we were windblown and dusty—and I, as usual, was badly sun-burned after driving all day with the top down. We only cleaned up a little and went down to dinner.

As we walked through the lobby, the hotel manager came up and said:

"Word is out that you are here, Mrs. Roosevelt, and a lot of people would like to meet you."

"I'm sorry," Mrs. Roosevelt said gently, "but we're tired and, as you see, somewhat travel-worn. We have to leave very early tomorrow morning. We'd like to be excused, if you please."

The hotel dining room had a wide picture window, with one of the most breath-taking views of snow-capped mountains I've ever seen. The dinner was good, and we enjoyed it immensely as we watched the rays of the setting sun turn the snowy mountain tops to rosy pink. We felt well-fed, relaxed and very contented as we started to leave the dining room.

But we stepped out into a lobby packed with people —the mayor of Bend at the head of the line. A reception.

Silently Mrs. Roosevelt handed me our keys. I was apt not to behave well under such circumstances, she had learned. And I went upstairs and left her.

Half an hour later I let her in. She came into my room, slammed the door behind her—something I'd never known her to do before, nor did I ever know her do it since that night—and sat down on my bed. On either cheek was a red spot. They used to appear that way when she was annoyed.

"Franklin was right!" she said.

"What do you mean?" I asked her.

"Franklin said I'd never get away with it," she replied, "and I can't."

She was silent for a moment. Then she sighed and added:

"From now on I shall travel as I'm supposed to travel, as the President's wife, and try to do what is expected of me."

Then she added defiantly:

"But there's one thing I will not do. I will not have a Secret Service man following me about. *Never!*"

Near the end of the closing chapter of her book *This I Remember* Mrs. Roosevelt wrote, some fifteen years later, these sentences:

"It was almost as though I had erected someone a little outside myself who was the President's wife. I was lost somewhere deep down inside myself. That is the way I lived and worked until I left the White House."